Birdies, Bogeys, & Bipolar Disorder

The Fight against Mental Illness
on and off the Green

MICHAEL WELLINGTON

RIVER GROVE
BOOKS

D1400534

Published by River Grove Books
Austin, TX
www.rivergrovebooks.com

Copyright ©2015 Michael Wellington

Distributed by River Grove Books

For ordering information or special discounts for bulk purchases, please contact River Grove Books at PO Box 91869, Austin, TX 78709, 512.891.6100.

Design and composition by Greenleaf Book Group
Cover design by Greenleaf Book Group
Cover image: ©iStock/golfladi; ©Shutterstock/Abel Tumik; ©Shutterstock/CrackerClips Stock Media; ©Shutterstock/Julia Ivantsova; ©Shutterstock/Dan Thornberg; ©Shutterstock/Mega Pixel; ©Shutterstock/ Ruslan Semichev

Cataloging-in-Publication data is available.

Print ISBN: 978-1-63299-064-8

eBook ISBN: 978-1-63299-065-5

Printed in the United States of America on acid-free paper

First Edition

This book is dedicated to Mom, Dad, Amy, and Kevin. You are the very definition of family. Your unconditional love and support allowed this book to happen and I am forever grateful for all of you.

This book is also dedicated to my amazing group of friends who each played their own role in helping me to respect the power of bipolar disorder. There is not enough space here to list all of your names but you know who you are. Thank you for believing in me when I didn't believe in myself.

"*Only you can work on you. Nobody can force you, and if you aren't ready, then you aren't ready, and no amount of open-armed encouragement is going to change that. You have to decide to help yourself, it's your choice.*"
—Dr. C. Robert Cloninger, MD, PhD

CONTENTS

FOREWORD

People often ask me what the difference is between bipolar I and bipolar II and the answer is, of course, one. Apparently, these are people who struggle with basic math, and I thought *I* was the one with the mental illness! Actually, if you are bipolar I, you aren't reading this or anything else; you're probably standing on a street corner somewhere wearing a canary-yellow toga, snatching imaginary fruit off an invisible tree, and yodeling the Brazilian national anthem in French—which is clearly not right, as most Brazilians speak Portuguese. Bipolar II, you see, is the inability to do anything at a rate of less than 8000%, all of the time, including feeling really fucking awful for no apparent reason. This gives most bipolar II sufferers the unfortunate characteristics of a person who, unmedicated, is unbearably enthusiastic, followed by an unimaginably sad identical twin in great physical pain. No two people have the exact same symptoms, but this is pretty much what it feels like.

Of course, part of the frustration of this mental illness is that allegedly normal people have no idea how you feel, and furthermore, you don't want them to, because the only way to know is to suffer also. This is why I feel sorry for my psychiatrist, because "He that would help must venture into the very fire that consumes me," which is a famous quote that I just made up on the fly. I know, it's fucking brilliant, but it comes hand in hand with the kind of stupidity that made me agree to write the foreword for this book in the first place. Writing is one of the things that really depresses me—too much like work for my liking.

What a party the search for the right medicine was—or so I am led to believe. Frankly, there were weeks and months during which I didn't know whether I was blown up or stuffed and even times when I couldn't find a liquor store that was five blocks from my house. And still is. . . . What eventually worked for me is a cocktail of Lamictal, Abilify, and enough Adderall a day to keep a 1200-pound grizzly bear awake for the winter.

This doesn't make me feel any good of course, as none of these drugs are any fun at all. On the contrary, they make me feel hollow and occasionally rob me of self-worth and dignity to the extent that, all too often, I simply have to be alone. However, these problems fade into insignificance when compared with the horror of the cold, dark place I hurtle toward if I stop taking them.

A human can live without everything except air to breathe, food and water to sustain, and hope—and without hope, depression will most certainly rob you of the other three. For the record, depressives are not cowards, and they don't die from suicide. Suicide is merely a side effect of a disease that swells around its victim like a malignant tumor and that can be just as deadly. Suicide is painless when compared with the agony that depressives can so often believe they are putting their loved ones through. And I just ended a sentence with a preposition, which depresses me again (but not enough to change it, apparently).

Like Michael, I will take my little handful of pills each day and be glad of the fact that when I am ill, there are people who love me and will take care of me. I have Dr. Art Aurazo, my family, my wife and my children, and the tiny paws, nose, and tongue of my small beagle. I have more friends than I deserve, and none of them but Art has the slightest idea of how I feel. That is the way I like it. And anyway, I have decided I am not going to be depressed any more. Instead, I am going to spend the rest of my life depressing other people. The very thought of this cheers me the fuck up immensely, and yet at the same time, it depresses me that I didn't think of it earlier.

And there you go. . . .

David Feherty
February 2015

ACKNOWLEDGMENTS

This book would not have become a reality without some Herculean efforts from some very special people.

A world of thanks goes to Nick Sansone, who saw the vision and importance of this project from the very beginning. You are a tremendous man for others.

Another debt of gratitude goes to Kevin Heaney, who infused life into the project at a critical time in the production process.

Many thanks to my writing coach and first editor, Christy Heady. Your expertise and faith in the story were essential when the book was in its infant stages.

And a special thanks to my friend David Feherty, who contributed the foreword to this book. You are a great American and a supreme example of someone who wins the battle against mental illness every day.

And thank you to all the wonderful professionals and editors and Greenleaf Book Group: Justin Branch, Brandy Savarese, Nathan True, Emilie Lyons, Carrie Jones, and Elizabeth Chenette.

I

THE FIRST EPISODE

*I'm familiar with that feeling of silence that comes with
a very imminent catastrophe, which you know you have
absolutely no control over a situation.*
—*Dave Matthews*

I WAS STRAPPED to a table with restraints over my arms, my chest, and my legs in a hospital emergency room in Fort Myers, Florida. I was fidgeting and restless; sweat poured down my face and panic raced through my mind as I tried to break through the confining straps. Nurses and doctors pinned me down against my will and screamed at me. I thought that I was going to die.

"Michael! Come on, Michael!"

Tubes running into my throat connected me to a machine pumping my stomach. I could only breathe through my nose, and I was beginning to see that light that people always claim to see when they are dying. It was getting brighter and brighter, and it seemed as if I was moving closer to it every second. As the light captured my full attention I finally stopped thrashing, but there was something tethering me to earth. It was the voices, yelling my name, conjuring visions of my past.

In one moment, it sounded as if they were cheering me on. They were eerily similar to the voices that encouraged me when I was a young boy competing in a swim meet, sprinting freestyle the length of a pool. In between breaths, I could hear the voices pushing me to swim faster and harder. The voices were yelling my name, rooting for me.

They were the voices of basketball fans, cheering on my high school team as we played to advance to the final four of our state tournament. I sat on the bench for almost the entire game because that was my role—I was a benchwarmer and I loved it. When I was finally called into the game, I had two assignments: play tough defense (get fouled) and make free throws. The pressure was intense, and I relished every second of it. At 1:14 remaining on the clock, I checked in at the scorer's table; with 1:12 left, I got the ball and was fouled. Walking up to the free-throw line, Michael Eveler, my best friend since the second grade, slapped me on the back and did what any best friend would do in that situation: He lied to me. He told me I was the best free-throw shooter on the team (even though he was our best free-throw shooter). As I stepped to the free-throw line, I could hear the crowd going wild. "Michael! Come on, Michael! Come on, Michael!" I made both free throws. One minute and twelve seconds later, we won the game.

"Come on, Michael! Michael! Michael, stay with us! Come on, Michael!"

But, in that moment in the ER, my bipolar mind could not distinguish the difference between the yells of high school sports fans urging me to victory and the desperate voices of people trying to save my life.

* * *

In the winter of 2001, I had just finished college and was chasing my dream of playing professional golf. Golf was my life.

The love affair began when I was little, accompanying my dad to the golf course. I remember being about four years old when he threw me in the green-side bunker next to him during one of his practice sessions at the golf course.

"Daddy, where are my toys?" I was used to playing with a shovel and Tonka Trucks in the sandbox at home.

"Here are your toys," he said, handing me a couple golf balls and a club.

I really fell in love with the game while watching Jack Nicklaus win his sixth Masters green jacket in an epic battle with Seve Ballesteros, Tom Kite, and Greg Norman when I was nine years old. My love grew even more when my golf idol, Fred Couples, held off Raymond Floyd to win the 1992 Masters.

I loved everything about golf. I loved the players, their caddies, and even the broadcasters, whose voices became burned on my brain. I recorded tournaments on VHS tapes and watched them over and over until I had them memorized. If Fred Couples and his caddie, Joe LaCava, were in a tournament broadcast on television, you could be sure that I was watching.

I made myself into a very good player by copying Couples's swing and tempo. While in college, I kept up the hard work, spending the majority of my time playing and practicing on the golf course, rather than attending class. In my junior year I made the all-American team with a victory in the NAIA Southeast Regional Championship. I tied for a medal at the national championship, losing in a sudden-death playoff for the individual title.

I had a lot to live for in the winter of 2001, but because I hadn't been taking my recently prescribed lithium every day my mind had turned on me.

I had been watching the Duke versus North Carolina basketball game, but as I tried to relax on my couch, I had this overwhelming feeling that someone was watching me and that they were trying to kill me. Every few minutes, I would leap up from the couch brandishing a golf club and run to the window to see who was watching me. I had never felt so paranoid, and I had no idea I had fallen into a mixed manic episode, in which the bipolar mind jumps rapidly between feeling depressed and worried to feeling euphoric and free.

What the fuck is happening to me? I was an all-American college golfer and the editor of my college newspaper. *What happened to my confidence and direction?*

* * *

A month or so before the paranoid episode, I had impulsively embarked on a 150-mile drive across Florida, from Fort Myers to Orlando, to challenge Tiger Woods. Woods, the best golfer in the history of the sport, was coming off what was arguably the greatest season ever for a professional golfer. I wanted to see his game up close and challenge him to play me.

Woods had won the 2000 US Open at Pebble Beach by fifteen shots, had set the low-scoring record while winning the 2000 British Open at St. Andrews, and had claimed his third major championship in a row by winning the 2000 PGA Championship in an epic playoff against Bob May at Valhalla, in Louisville, Kentucky. I was still an amateur golfer with one college victory under my belt—not the type of golf resume to be on the same course as Woods. I had met Woods in the summer of 1999, when I worked at the Maroon Creek Club, in Aspen, Colorado. He had been very nice, and I imagined that he would welcome a challenge.

I don't give a fuck if he is the best player on the planet; I'm not afraid of him. He's only a man.

When I arrived at the entrance to Woods's neighborhood, the security guard told me that he wasn't home. So I drove to Disney World, "The Happiest Place on Earth." I remember pulling my car off to the side of the road at the entrance and crying uncontrollably. Then, I turned my car around and drove all the way back to Fort Myers. To this day, I have no idea why I was crying, but it wouldn't be the last time.

A week later, I spent more than $2,000 on framed posters, autographed photographs and balls, bobbleheads, and figurines at a sports memorabilia shop. I purchased these items to display in the apartment that I was renting for $600 per month on a six-month lease. It was my first apartment out of college; it should have been filled with macaroni and cheese, peanut butter, and ramen noodles, not autographed posters of Reggie Jackson and Brett Favre. I bought my roommate an expensive golf club for no reason. I paid a handyman $200 to fix the kitchen sink when he asked for only $50 to do the job. I was literally giving money away, even though I didn't have any golf sponsors supplementing my income at that point. Money was tight, but I was spending like a pro.

My episodes—challenging Tiger Woods, the spending spree, functioning on little-to-no sleep, and exhibiting strange behavior during phone calls with my family—prompted my parents to visit me in Florida. They took me to a doctor who explained that I was exhibiting symptoms of bipolar disorder and prescribed lithium to manage it. I didn't argue with the diagnosis, but I didn't agree that I needed the medication. It seemed simple enough at the time: Don't take it. I even hid the bottle.

I don't need that lithium. That drug may hurt my golf game. It could ruin my touch around the greens or wreck my confidence with my putter. I was a great player in college and never took that medicine. Fuck the medicine. So what I may have bipolar disorder, but I don't need medicine. I can handle it on my own.

My ego and inexperience with bipolar disorder were very dangerous enemies to my health, finally resulting in the mixed manic episode. The illness jumbled my thoughts so badly that I swung rapidly from believing that I didn't need the medicine at all to thinking that I needed to catch up on all the pills I had been skipping for weeks.

* * *

Remembering the lithium, I raced to my bathroom and searched for the full bottle that I had buried in a drawer. I emptied half the contents into my hand and shoved the pills into my mouth, chasing them with handfuls of water from the bathroom faucet. The water ran out of my mouth, getting all over my face and my shirt. A few stray pills hit the floor as I tried to cram them into my mouth.

I must have swallowed twenty or twenty-five pills. And, for a moment, I was at ease. I had done the right thing.

Then, as I sat on the edge of my bed, the reality of what I had done hit me. I had made a horrible decision. Panic choked me.

That was too many. I took too many. Fuck. The pills are going to kill me now.

I jumped up and raced into my roommate's bedroom, telling him what I had done. Then I sprinted out of the apartment, running for my life. My roommate, on the phone with a mutual friend when I dashed into his room, thankfully realized he needed to call 911 and my parents.

I ran until the awful feeling of someone chasing me wore off. When I reached a vacant parking lot a few blocks from my apartment, I finally felt safe enough to stop and return home. A police car was waiting for me. I was handcuffed and put into the back of the squad car to wait until an ambulance arrived. The officer pulled me from the back of the car and escorted me to the back door of the ambulance, where I told the medic that I had just taken a handful of lithium pills. The handcuffs came off, and the restraints went on.

* * *

"Stay with us, Michael! Come on, Michael! Michael! Come on, Michael!"

The doctors and nurses continued to scream my name as tubes blocked my throat and vomit oozed from of the corners of my mouth and ran down my chin.

This was the first time that my bipolar disorder had tricked me into doing something that put my life in jeopardy. I was in the hospital getting 6,000 milligrams of lithium pumped out of my stomach.

"Michael! Great job, Michael! Come on, Michael! Atta boy, Michael!"

The voices were cheering me back from the abyss and relaxed me enough that I allowed them to do their jobs. They got the lithium out of my stomach just in time—any longer and the lithium would have entered my bloodstream and stopped my heart. As they pulled the tubes out of my throat, I felt relieved, even though I still had vomit dripping from my chin and my hair was soaked in sweat. I was exhausted, but still in the throes of mania.

Before I could even get my bearings, I was ushered out of the hospital and into the backseat of a white Buick. I had no clue where I was going, and I didn't argue.

The driver was a heavy-set woman wearing a baseball cap, her curly hair making the hat sit very high on her head. The woman in the passenger seat was small, and my view of her head was blocked by the headrest. I remember the radio blaring oldies during the hour-long drive; the volume was very loud. The women didn't say much to each other or me during the drive, and I made no attempt to communicate with them. I just listened to the music and looked out the window. With my mania in full tilt, the obvious choice seemed to be to look at this as a new adventure. So, I just went with it.

When the car stopped, I noticed we were outside a large building that resembled an abandoned warehouse. Only it wasn't a warehouse, it was the Florida state mental hospital in Sarasota, but I didn't know that then. I spent the first six hours there by myself in a single room. I was exhausted, but too scared to sleep. I hadn't slept in the past four days, but my mania prevented me from even a few minutes of rest. This experience had gone from a new adventure to a terrifying experience.

An orderly who was every bit of six foot five and 300-plus pounds finally opened the door and escorted me into the general population of the hospital. There were approximately thirty people in the main living area, ranging in age from as young as twenty to as old as sixty. Some were catatonic in chairs and on couches; others were silently curled up in a corner like they were hiding from the light of day. There were several people talking out loud to themselves as they stared out windows or at me. A woman in her thirties, wearing a black robe, sat Indian-style in the middle of the floor singing Christmas carols. It was a frightening scene.

A weathered and gray-haired man in his late fifties, wearing a red robe over polka-dot pajamas and brown velvet slippers, approached and told me he was Elvis Presley. I humored him and listened to his rambling. He was so close as he spoke that I thought my eyebrows were going to catch fire from his rancid breath. His teeth were crooked, and he was missing his lower two incisors. As Elvis regaled me with stories about his albums and the famous friends that would be visiting him, I began to believe that I had died and been sent to rot in hell. I actually thought, *Maybe this is what Elvis looks like in hell.* On earth, he had been a handsome, dark-haired rock star whom women adored. No woman would have gone within ten feet of this guy.

After Elvis finished, I joined a table of people that looked like they were around my age. I attempted to talk with some of them, but no one was very receptive. One girl even turned her back on me as I tried to start a conversation. I hadn't seen myself in a mirror since being in this place—maybe I looked different here, too.

After more than an hour in the main living area, I finally convinced one of the nurses into allowing me a phone call. I dialed my parents' house in St. Louis. I didn't know where I was, but when my mom answered I knew I must not be in hell.

"Are you okay?" Mom asked me.

"Yes," I told her. "But I am in some sort of jail, and I don't know where it is. Am I in Florida?"

"I don't know," she admitted. "Can you put a nurse on the phone so I can talk with her?"

I passed the phone to a nurse so she could talk to my mom, feeling a sense of relief. I knew my mom would do her best to get me out of there.

The next hours in that hellhole passed so slowly. I hadn't been given any medication and hadn't slept in what seemed like forever. I had not been evaluated by any doctors since arriving, and my mania was beginning to boil. I become mean and surly in a manic state, and I was becoming more edgy by the minute. I began berating the nurses and orderlies, shouting orders at them and insulting them for no reason.

"I want to use the phone again! Take me to the room with the phones!" I demanded.

When the nurses paid no attention to me, I screamed in one nurse's face, "Take me in there, you dumb bitch! I want to make a call—now!"

I was nearing acute mania. The insults were becoming louder and more obnoxious. The inner ugliness of bipolar disorder was taking over my external world.

The nurses and orderlies didn't wait long to sedate me and lock me into an eight-by-eight solitary confinement cell with a cot and a window to the nurses' station. On the opposite side of the room was a door with a small square window at eye level that looked out into a hallway. I was literally thrown into the cell by a male nurse; after spouting off the way I had, I probably deserved it.

The sedatives slowed me down, but my paranoia began to cause hallucinations. Over and over, I saw a man in his forties sticking his red face and white hair into the square window of the door. He mocked me and made faces at me. I tried to bang down the door to get to him, to no avail.

Eventually, I was passed a sandwich and a cup of water through the nurses' station window into my cell, which had a small opening at the bottom big enough to send food and drink through. Starving, I took a bite of the sandwich. It was turkey and Swiss cheese, slathered in mayonnaise. I hate mayonnaise; even the thought of it makes me sick to my stomach. I spit it out and guzzled the water.

I was completely confused from the mania, the sedatives, exhaustion, and dehydration and lost all track of time. I had to use the restroom so badly that I was banging on the window to the nurses' station, but no one would let me out. So, I used the water cup. It overflowed and urine got on the floor, but I didn't care. I tried my best to sleep after that, but the cot was too small for me.

When I woke up, my brain felt as if it had been removed and scrambled in a frying pan. I was so thirsty that I grabbed the full cup from the floor. It took me a good five seconds to realize that I was drinking my own urine. I spewed it all over the cell. I have never felt more alone than I did at that moment.

Unbeknownst to me, my dad was on his way to Florida to get me out of the hospital. The first time he was allowed to see me I was a drooling mess, having been administered massive amounts of sedatives. I remember sitting across the table from him hearing him speak to me as if I were an infant. I couldn't get any words out. It was as if my tongue had been taken hostage.

The laws in Florida do not favor the patient and made it very difficult for my dad to spring me from the hospital. Luckily, my dad is an excellent salesman. After five hours of negotiating with officials and signing half a dozen insurance forms freeing the hospital of any liability, I was released into my dad's care. The hospital gave him medication to keep me calm on the plane ride back to St. Louis; it worked—I can only remember bits and pieces of the trip.

When I woke up, in my own bed, I finally felt safe. I wondered whether it had just been a bad dream. It all seemed so surreal. My mom explained what had happened and helped me remember the events that had led me back to their kitchen five states away. It hadn't been a dream.

We found ourselves in uncharted waters. None of us had any clue about the power of bipolar disorder, but we were learning quickly.

My entire personality had been turned upside down. The high, manic side of bipolar disorder had chewed me up in Florida and spit me out in St. Louis. Now the depression was looming: I had no desire to play golf. I was over it. I was going to quit. I even blamed golf for what happened to me. Bipolar disorder had driven me away from golf, my heart and soul. Still, I had no idea about the power of the depression that was lurking around the corner for me. I had not yet learned to respect bipolar disorder.

THE FOURTEEN CLUBS

At the end of the book, I've listed a set of tools to support the bipolar mind, which I call the *Fourteen Clubs*. Consistently using these tools has helped me avoid repeating situations like my overdose on medication. If I had been following a routine and regularly taking my meds, I would have been more stable, able to think more clearly, and wouldn't have missed the doses that I tried to catch up on. Using the Fourteen Clubs or coming up with your own tools for a healthy mind can help you control bipolar disorder.

GETTING HEALTHY AT Q-SCHOOL

Life is either a daring adventure or nothing.
—*Helen Keller*

EVEN THOUGH I was safe in St. Louis, I was far from healthy. I still wasn't keen on taking my lithium, but my mom was going to make sure I didn't miss a single pill. Every morning, she waited for me in the kitchen with my lithium pills and a glass of orange juice. My dad would be there too, to ensure that the medicine made its way to the bottom of my belly.

The lithium kept the mania away, but I faced a new challenge: depression. One of the reasons that bipolar disorder sufferers have such a high suicide rate is because the depressive side of the disorder leads them into the deepest, darkest side of depression from which they can't find a way out.

Until the episode in Florida, I had never felt a single twinge of depression. My life had been filled with joy and happiness. But, just as sure as spring turns to summer and summer turns to fall, bipolar manic episodes become depression when the mania calms down. This is a cycle I would come to know well in my battle with bipolar disorder.

With the lithium in my system for two weeks, my mania was replaced by the deepest physical and mental depression. It siphoned the life out of me and held me in its iron grip. I thought depression was something that happened to kids whose parents were divorced, or something that only happened to the weak minded. I never thought it could touch me.

For the next three weeks, it would take me half an hour to work myself out of bed every morning, my legs and arms feeling too heavy to move. In order to get out of bed, I would literally force myself to fall onto the floor. From there I'd struggle to my feet. I never made it out before ten o'clock in the morning. Most twenty-three-year-olds bounce out of bed—or, at least, emerge upright—all I could muster was to flail myself onto the floor.

Eventually, I began to use fitness to pull myself out of the depression. I started walking around my neighborhood in the morning. After a week of walking, I jogged. By the third week, I was able to mix jogging with sprinting. Fitness was the catalyst that finally pulled me out of the deep depression. I began to feel a little better, my energy levels were on the rise, and the lithium made my moods more stable. I ate regular, square meals, which also helped my mental state, and my friends took turns getting me back into normal social settings.

* * *

By the end of March I was better, but I had very little desire to play golf.

Every April for the previous five years, I would begin my preparation for the US Open qualifying rounds held during the first part of May. But, I didn't feel right to play golf. Golfers must be intimately aware of how they feel and what their body is telling them; in order to play great golf, you must be creative and clear minded. In the spring of 2001, my lithium-flooded mind was telling me that my body was off—not able to swing a club. Although my health and well-being had vastly improved, I felt different than I had in the past. I had played ten months out of every year for the past five years—golf had been a huge part of my life. But, depression owned me and kept me from the sport I loved most.

I continued to be in denial that I needed to be medicated, but my friends and family were relentless about me taking it. I had a stubborn ego like most kids in their early twenties, but the support of my friends kept me going. My parents, knowing how important it was to my well-being to play golf again, connected me with a sports psychologist, whom I began to see. He later told me that as I walked out of his office after the first session, a golf tee fell out of my pocket, and he knew that it was only a matter of time before I would get back on the golf course. April turned to May, and May turned to June, and finally my interest in golf began to return, mostly because I watched the 2001 US Open, held at Southern Hills Country Club, in Tulsa, Oklahoma, on television.

I knew the course well.

* * *

In the spring of 1998, I competed in the NAIA National Championship at Southern Hills, playing four competitive rounds and making great memories of Tulsa, the tournament, and the course.

I had the greatest par save of my life at Southern Hills, on the sixteenth hole—a 495-yard par four that plays uphill on the tee shot and downhill on the approach to the green. My tee shot found the right side of the fairway, leaving me 210 yards to the hole with my second shot. I took too much club on my approach and smoked a three-iron shot twenty yards over the green, forcing me to manufacture a save.

I couldn't play a high soft shot, because there were thick tree branches just above my head and stretching all the way to the bunker separating me from the back edge of the green. My first option was to skip a low shot through the sand, making the ball spill onto the green. But it was an extremely risky shot that would be nearly impossible to pull off. The sand in the bunker would most likely take all the momentum out of the shot, landing the ball in the trap.

My second option was to use the cart path, just a few feet short of the bunker. I could try for a low shot under the tree branches, landing the ball on the cart path and allowing it to bounce over the bunker and onto the green. That was my shot, I decided, and it came off exactly as planned. I chose a seven iron and played a low chip shot. The ball stayed under the branches, hit the cart path just right, and carried perfectly over the trap. It landed a few feet onto the green and spilled another forty feet before coming to rest only ten feet to the right of the hole, which was cut on the front third of the putting surface. I made the putt and ran to the next tee as if I had stolen something.

* * *

Most people remember the 2001 US Open at Southern Hills because Retief Goosen and Stewart Cink had both made a mess on the seventy-second green, knocking Cink out of the tournament and forcing Goosen into an eighteen-hole playoff the next day with Mark Brooks. I caddied for Brooks at Glen Frey's charity event in Aspen during the summer of 1999, the year after I competed in the NAIA National Championship. Brooks was an awesome guy to caddy for, and I was definitely rooting for him in the playoff at Southern Hills. Goosen rode a scalding hot putter to his first US Open title, and watching that tournament reawakened my passion for golf.

I had been taking my meds every day for four months and I was eating right, exercising regularly, and keeping my alcohol intake to a minimum. I was healthy.

So I picked up my sticks.

I entered my first tournament of 2001, the St. Louis District Amateur Championship at Meadowbrook Country Club in July. It is the oldest amateur tournament in St. Louis and boasts PGA Tour players in its list of champions. I had even caddied for my dad in this event when I was ten years old. The format of the tournament had been the same for decades. The top thirty-two qualifiers from stroke play would be put into a bracket for match play. Match-play golf has nothing to do with stroke play or cumulative score; it's one-on-one. The lowest score wins the hole.

Although I hadn't been practicing, I was itching to compete. I was rusty, but I hit enough good shots during the stroke play to get some of my feel back. I snuck through the qualifying round and secured the lucky thirteen seed in the ranking of the top thirty-two qualifiers from stroke play. I would be tested in my first match.

First I played Mark Norman, a seasoned local amateur. He was in his early forties and certainly had the advantage in experience. I was one hole down with two holes to play heading to the seventeenth hole, a par three. I played a laser beam 171-yard seven-iron tee shot to within inches of the hole to square the match. We tied on the eighteenth hole and headed into sudden death. On the first extra hole, I hooked my tee shot to send it out of bounds when it suddenly hit the curb of the cart path and bounced back from disaster into the middle of the fairway. This is easily the luckiest break of my entire golf career. When Norman saw my ball finish in a good position, his shoulders slumped. It took the wind right out of his sails. He hit his tee shot into the fairway bunker, landing underneath the lip of the trap so he couldn't advance his ball. I made a par to his bogey and won the match one up in nineteen holes.

I was back in my element, and I loved it. It felt good to be in the heat of tournament golf and that win kicked my confidence into high gear. I had a smile on my face that hadn't been there for months.

My second-round match was against Scott Fann, a high school teammate who had been like a little brother to me. He was on a hot streak in the summer of 2001 and was arguably the best player in St. Louis that year. I would have my hands full with him. But I had always been a strong match-play competitor, and this time was no different. I made six birdies in fifteen holes and won the match 4 and 3. It was a good victory for me. I continued to play well, and my confidence grew.

I faced Kevin Goalby in my third-round match. His father, Bob, won the 1968 Masters tournament, and Kevin was a tenacious competitor who played for the University of Georgia. I played with him in the summer of 2000 and enjoyed it immensely. I liked his fiery demeanor. He pushed me to the sixteenth hole, where I finally put him away 3 and 2 with a wild birdie from the right trees. That shot secured my move on to the semifinals, where I would face Tim Riley.

Riley was the defending champion of the event and the type of player who made lots of birdies. But my putter was hot against Riley and the hole on every green looked like the size of Lake Michigan; I made every putt I looked at in that match and played my best golf of the tournament against him. I birdied five holes on the front nine, added two more on the back nine, and beat him 4 and 3, earning a berth in the final match.

The final match, contested over thirty-six holes, would be a real challenge. I faced David Johnson out of Norwood Hills Country Club, home to many great players. He was used to facing top-quality competition every weekend. With fifteen years on me, it would once again be a matchup of experience against youth.

My sixteen-year-old brother Kevin caddied for me, making it an even more special round. He had been waiting for me at the airport when I arrived home after my first manic episode, so it meant a lot for me to have him on my bag. He was a great caddie, and he talked me into a very sensible decision on our thirty-fourth hole with a one-up lead.

The hole was a short, tight, drivable par four that measured 325 yards. But hitting with a driver could be trouble, with thick trees just a few yards to either side of the fairway. The green was also guarded by a deep bunker. My natural instinct was to be aggressive and to try to drive the green, but Kevin wouldn't let me hit the driver. He guarded my bag like a watchdog, going so far as to use his body to block me from grabbing the driver.

"You're gonna have to wrestle me to get the driver," he said.

"Fuck you. Give me the fuckin' driver," I said quietly so the gallery couldn't hear my profanity.

"Michael, you are one up and Johnson is going to play safe, too. There is no advantage to hitting a driver. Make him make birdies to beat you. You are in control because you have the lead," he explained.

"All right," I conceded. "Give me the five iron." I hit the fairway and made a sensible par with a wedge shot onto the green. Johnson had a twenty-foot putt for birdie that lipped out.

As we came to the par-three thirty-fifth hole, I was clinging to my one-up advantage. I played a seven iron to fifteen feet below the hole. With Johnson missing his par-saving putt from twenty feet, I had two putts to win the match. I left my birdie putt two feet from the hole, and Johnson conceded the putt and the match. I won 2 and 1.

After shaking hands with Johnson, I met my dad on the back of the green, where we hugged in celebration. I think we both cried during that embrace. Just a few hours earlier, he had really saved the day by bringing my lithium to the sixth hole. In my excitement for the match, I had forgotten to take it that morning. He admitted a few days later that, when he first saw me in the hospital back in Sarasota, he thought I would never return to the confident and well-spoken young man he had raised. But in that moment, five months later, I had overcome mania and solitary confinement in a mental hospital to make it back to the sport we both loved with a significant amateur championship win in my hometown.

Victory at the St. Louis District Amateur was my first significant finish in a golf tournament since my junior year of college. I entered two more events that summer, the Metropolitan Amateur Championship at Gateway National Golf Links where I shot 76–69–69 to finish in the top ten, and the Jim Jackson Invitational at Algonquin Golf Club where I shot 70–71 to finish runner-up to Scott Edwards, another strong St. Louis amateur.

My bipolar disorder seemed to vanish as my golf game rose from the dead. The confidence I felt on the golf course was fueling my feeling of being unstoppable, so I decided to attack one of the biggest challenges in golf: the PGA Tour Q-School. If you had asked me at the beginning of June 2001 if I was going to Q-School, I would have laughed at you. Now I was jumping into golf's ultimate pressure cooker with my old college-kid swagger and a boatload of confidence. Books have been written about much more experienced players than me having disasters at this event, but I was ready to go.

In 2001 the primary way to get on the PGA Tour was through Q-School, a grueling three-stage, twelve-round qualifier hosted at nineteen courses across the country. The top 20 percent of players move on from the four-round first stage; the top 20 percent advance from the four-round second stage into the finals, in which they join players who were exempted from the six qualifying rounds. The top twenty-five finishers at the final stage earn PGA Tour cards for the next year. Players finishing twenty-sixth through seventy-fifth gain status on the Web.com Tour, the PGA Tour's brother circuit where the talent is just as deep, but the prize money is less. A player who wins an event on the PGA Tour collects somewhere in the neighborhood of a million dollars; on the Web.com Tour, a winner receives closer to $100,000.

My dad decided to join me at Q-School. My little brother Kevin couldn't take a week off school to caddy for me, so my good friend Johnny Mullin came along to carry my bag. Together, the three of us made the six-hour drive from St. Louis to the Old Fort Golf Club, a very flat municipal golf course in Murfreesboro, Tennessee.

I got a taste of just how talented Q-School competitors are in my first practice round. Most practice rounds consist of playing a few extra shots, with a different ball, on each hole as well as making extra putts on each green, to get a feel for the course. Mullin had caddied for me before, so we were focused on taking the lay of the land when, on the sixth tee box, he pulled me aside to share some important information about my partner in the twosome, Steve Gilley.

"Steve has birdied four of the first five holes and has only been playing one ball on each hole," he mentioned.

I asked, "Are you sure?" I hadn't realized it because I was hitting a lot of extra shots of my own.

"He birdied one, two, four, and five and has only played one ball the entire time," Mullin explained.

This was not good news. I should have noticed that, but I had been distracted by our running baseball banter. As a Cardinals fan, I couldn't ignore that he was an Atlanta Braves fan.

"Well, shit," I said. "Let's stay out of his way for the rest of the day and see how low he can go."

When a player is taking it really low in a round of golf, the cardinal rule is "Don't talk about it." It's very much the same as when a major-league pitcher has a no-hitter going—you don't say a word.

Gilley stayed hot through the front nine, making three more birdies at seven, eight, and nine to shoot seven under par on the front side. My dad, who was following our group, said to me on the walk to the tenth tee, "Did that guy just shoot 30 on the front?"

"Twenty-nine," I corrected him.

"Keep him loose on the back nine," he advised. "Let's see how low he can go."

Gilley stalled a bit on ten, eleven, and twelve, making three pars in a row. He recovered slightly with a birdie on thirteen to go to eight under for the day, with five holes to go. Mullin and I started doing the math while walking down the fourteenth fairway. Mullin figured that if Gilley birdied the rest of the holes, he would shoot 59 for the round.

Gilley chipped in from short of the fourteenth green to move to nine under for the round. We all celebrated when his ball disappeared into the cup. He made an easy birdie on the fifteenth hole, reaching par five in two mammoth shots. He was ten under, with just three holes to go.

He threw a dart to within two feet of the hole to sixteen and went to eleven under. I had never seen a game like this. He made a scrambling par at seventeen; no doubt a score of 59 was on his mind at that point. He needed to hole a shot from the fairway at eighteen, so we kept him preoccupied with small talk at the tee. He hit his approach to six feet from 147 yards and made the putt for an incredible twelve under par score of 60. We all shook hands and left the green marveling at what an amazing round he had just put together.

"One day too early." Gilley lamented, because it was a practice round.

"Welcome to Q-School!" my dad said, laughing, as Mullin and I headed toward the car.

The following morning, I woke up ready to play and got to the golf course feeling pretty good. But as we got closer and closer to my tee time, anxiety kicked in and I grew more and more nervous by the minute. My heart was in my throat, and it beat so hard that it felt like it had set up shop next to my Adam's apple.

I had never been as nervous as I was when Mullin and I arrived at the first tee. I felt more anxiety on that tee box than I had facing the psychiatric ward in a mental institution. It's amazing that a game, played with a little white ball and some sticks in a bag, could get my adrenaline pumping more than being locked up against my will.

I teed up my ball, with both my hands and legs trembling. As hundreds of thoughts raced through my mind I hit the ugliest snap hook you can imagine. The ball went sixty yards left of the fairway, out of bounds and into the parking lot. That was my "welcome to Q-School" moment.

My anger at the bad shot was off the charts but I didn't express it outwardly by throwing my club or cursing, like some players. Anger was a poison that I kept down, because it was important to me to retain a calm and cool demeanor like Fred Couples. Still, whether expressed or contained, anger is the opposite of focus, and I had lost my focus. I played on to shoot a disappointing 81 after that opening blunder. I followed that with rounds of 80, 75, and 75, to miss qualifying by a mile.

Q-School exposed my lack of maturity and made clear that anger sabotaged my brain and prevented me from focusing on the shot at hand. Instead, I obsessed over the bad shot that I already played. Q-School gave me my first tutorial on the vast differences between amateur and professional golf. But I learned that I needed to stop getting mad and work on getting better—that would be the key to my future success. My dad said it best, "Even though you didn't score very well, any of those days competing in that tournament sure beat any days in a hospital." He was relentlessly positive and exactly right. Since then, whenever I have gotten down on myself for not making a cut in a tournament or not making a paycheck, I always remember: *Any day playing tournament golf is better than a day locked in a psych ward.*

Gilley missed the cut, too. It's hard to believe that a guy who shot 60 one day before the tournament didn't advance to the next stage, but it's a good example of how golf can change from day to day.

Missing at Q-School for the first time was humbling; I had lots of work ahead. My next challenge was to return to Florida and begin my professional career. I thought that my bipolar disorder was also behind me, for good.

THE FOURTEEN CLUBS

I managed to remain relatively healthy and free of bipolar symptoms during this period because I stayed on my medication and created a routine that included a healthy diet and exercise. My dad bringing my medication to the golf course is an example of the support my parents have always shown me, and it likely saved me from a manic episode.

Golf has been especially important to me. Training keeps me physically healthy, and regularly doing something I love—especially something that has a built-in routine of its own—keeps my mind and body occupied. It doesn't make me immune to anxiety or frustration, but it helps me avoid mania and depression.

3

HEALTH AND SEASONING

Every artist was first an amateur.
—Ralph Waldo Emerson

IN LATE 2001, I got lucky. A good friend of my dad's gave me $25,000 to begin my golf career, allowing me to move back to Florida for the winter to work on my game and to caddie for extra money. I was excited to go back, hoping this time would be better. I decided to head to Jupiter, on the east coast, since Fort Myers, on the west coast, hadn't been too great for me.

Courtney and Mike, whom I'd met a few summers before, were going to room with me. They were pillars in my support system. For anyone battling a mental illness, a support system is just as important as consistently taking your meds. They were both familiar with my condition and knew that I'd had an intense episode in February. Courtney and Mike always made me feel comfortable about my illness, to the point that we'd often poke fun at some of the strange things that it had caused me to do. Teasing was one way they could remind me to stay on top of taking my medication without being too serious. Most people with bipolar disorder take themselves much too seriously; making fun of the illness—about the strangeness of the disease—can be a powerful coping mechanism.

* * *

By the beginning of 2002, my life had returned to relative normalcy. I was playing a mini tour sponsored by the Florida Panthers hockey franchise. I played four events on the Florida Panthers Tour (FPT), missing every cut, but I learned just how strong the competition is in lower-level professional golf.

During the remainder of 2002, I played on a few different tours and tournaments to prepare myself for a second crack at Q-School. My poor first showing had motivated me to improve, and I was relentless in my efforts. I spent hours in the gym and really focused on improving my short game. And I chased my lithium pills with a glass of Florida orange juice every morning. Although I continued to drink alcohol, I wasn't blacking out or suffering from too many hangovers. The relative control helped my bipolar disorder stay in its cage.

After playing on the FPT through the winter and early spring, I went north to play on the Stewart and Stewart Tour, which began in Florida and then traveled into Alabama, Georgia, and the Carolinas. I played seven events on that circuit during the spring and early summer of 2002, again missing every cut and burning through what I had left of the $25,000. Professional golf is obnoxiously expensive: Entry fees, hotels, caddies, gas, and food all add up quickly, especially when you aren't winning tournaments or making cuts.

* * *

In early March, I aced the fifth hole at Stonebridge Golf and Country Club in Boynton Beach, Florida, where a friend of mine was a teaching professional. It was my first hole in one.

The fifth hole at Stonebridge is a 185-yard par three with deep bunkers guarding the front of the green. When I hit my tee shot, I hit it flush, and the six-iron shot went straight for the flagstick, landed about eight feet short of the cup, and rolled right into the hole. We all began screaming and yelling.

Gary Pohrer, my college teammate playing with me that day, picked me up and squeezed the breath out of me with a bear hug.

"You sonovabitch!" he screamed as he shook me like a ragdoll.

I had never felt adrenaline like that before; it was an intoxicating rush.

Six months later, lightning struck again. On a scorching and humid August morning in St. Louis, I was playing in a father–son foursome at

Westborough Country Club with my dad and our friends Pete Benoist, Sr., and his son, Pete, Jr.

I wasn't playing well and was in a bad mood as we approached the ninth hole, a 195-yard par three. I had just made three bogeys in a row and I was sweating so much that it looked like I had just jumped into a pool, my clothes dark with moisture. I played first, choosing my five iron to lead off. When I made contact, I could feel that it wasn't a pure strike, but I knew I got a lot of the ball. Because I didn't catch the ball flush; it had no spin, so when it landed, it bounced forward onto the green and rolled about twenty feet directly into the hole. Another ace! We all watched the ball crash into the flagstick and go in. That shot renewed the life in our group, and sent high fives flying all over the ninth tee.

Just a month later, in September, I made a third hole-in-one in seven months. I was playing with my friend Gary Pohrer again, his brother Robert, and Tim Missey in a charity event at the Links at Dardenne, in St. Charles, Missouri. The seventeenth hole at Dardenne is a 130-yard par three. I was last to play in our group and hit with my fifty-two-degree gap wedge. My ball flew right over the flag, landing ten feet behind the hole and spun backward into the jar.

"That looks really good! That's going in! It's in!" Missey yelled as the ball disappeared into the cup.

Our group went ballistic.

"Wellington, you bastard!" Gary screamed.

Instead of picking me up in a bear hug as he had done the last time, Gary tackled me and we rolled down a small hill next to the tee box. That intoxicating adrenaline rush raced through my body again. It is the only feeling I have ever known that is more electric than a manic episode, but it only lasts for about ten minutes and a manic episode can last for weeks at a time. It was great momentum heading into Q-School.

* * *

After missing eleven cuts in a row at the beginning of my professional career, I entered the 2002 Gateway Masters at Bogey Hills Country Club, just outside of St. Louis. The Gateway Masters has a great history: Some of the its champions include Payne Stewart, Hal Sutton, and John Daly. I began the fifty-four-hole event with back-to-back rounds of 72 to make the cut safely by three shots.

After lunch I took a look at the scoreboard. The second-round score next to my name—71—was wrong. In tournament golf, it is the player's responsibility to check his or her own score on each hole and to make sure the scorecard is correct before signing it. I immediately went to the scoring area to see if I had made a mistake in the addition of my scorecard.

I had. The score was a birdie in the small box for the fifteenth hole. I had made a par four. It wasn't a mathematical error by the scorekeepers but an error that I had made by not checking my hole-by-hole scores carefully enough. I had to disqualify myself from the tournament for signing an incorrect scorecard. The disappointment was deflating.

It was a tough lesson to learn, but I wouldn't be able to sleep at night if I hadn't owned up to the infraction—I have always taken the rules of golf very seriously. Anyone who lives with bipolar disorder must hold themselves accountable and take the proper steps to remain healthy. At this point in my journey, there was no question that I respected the integrity of the game of golf, even though I had not yet learned the proper respect for bipolar disorder. Because I had put my health at the top of my priority list, I was convinced that the highs and lows of the disorder were far behind me. But bipolar disorder never goes away. It can push you to great highs and drag you to the depths of suicide within a matter of hours if you don't respect it. People who respect the game of golf can improve their play. The same thing is true with bipolar disorder: If you respect the seriousness of the disease, you can fight against it. But if you don't, it will haunt you and tangle up your mind.

* * *

I was not able to secure the $4,000 I needed to go to Q-School in 2002. So, instead of going to the tournament in 2002, I took a construction job in St. Louis.

My new plan was to work construction from October through the end of December and then move to Scottsdale, Arizona, to continue my golf career. I would have to wait another year for my chance to go through the

Q-School process. For players who are working their way up the professional golf ladder, Q-School is like the Super Bowl, so it hurt to sit out in 2002. But I was healthy and eighteen months removed from any sort of bipolar issues. I was taking my medicine every day, and my well-being was very good.

After working construction for three months in the cold of the St. Louis winter, my mind was clear, and I was hungry to make serious improvements on my golf game, which needed lots of work. My old friend John Stahlschmidt had just taken a job in Arizona to work as a golf instructor at the TPC of Scottsdale, the host course for the PGA Tour's Phoenix Open. John and I played against each other in high school. He played at the University of Alabama. In Arizona I worked with him on my swing—teaching the swing is his passion—and began to see improvement. The weather in Arizona was ideal to get in good work on my game—bright sunshine, perfect blue skies, warm days, and zero humidity. Sunny, warm weather can be extremely good for the psyche and it helped both my mood and my golf tremendously. My hard work was about to pay a small dividend.

* * *

My first paycheck during my time in Arizona came from playing on the Pepsi Tour, a mini tour that travels through California, Nevada, and Arizona. My first event was in Scottsdale at the Talking Stick Golf Club.

After the last round, I called my dad from the parking lot of a restaurant.

"Dad, I finally made a paycheck!" I was proud.

"What are you gonna do with the earnings?" he asked me.

"Pay the rent," I confessed.

I shot 69–69 in the two-day event for a paycheck of $710 at Talking Stick. Finances were very tight at the time and I really did need that rent money.

* * *

I played three more events on the Pepsi Tour in early 2003, making one more cut and an even smaller paycheck, but playing consistently well. I used the Pepsi Tour to sharpen my game so I could perform well at US Open Local Qualifying, which is usually held in the first two weeks of May.

I returned to St. Louis in mid-April to prepare for the US Open qualifying round at WingHaven Country Club, about forty-five minutes west of downtown St. Louis. The course is a par seventy-two designed by Jack Nicklaus. I have always liked Nicklaus courses because I enjoy hitting my tee shots with a left-to-right fade, which Nicklaus also did and incorporated into each of his designs.

I recruited my brother to caddie for me at WingHaven—the first time I had had Kevin on the bag since our victory at the St. Louis District Amateur two years earlier. I felt like I had my good luck charm with me again. Every great caddie has a sixth sense about when to offer advice and when to keep silent, and Kevin was particularly good at that.

The US Open local qualifier is always eighteen holes of stroke play. Advancing through the local qualifying secures you a spot at the sectional qualifier, which is thirty-six holes in one day. If you advance through that stage, you play in the US Open.

I had an early tee time at WingHaven, and it was raining and wet. I wore three layers, including a black Gore-Tex rain suit over everything, to stay warm and dry during my warm-up. My brother kept a dry towel dangling from the spokes of our umbrella for me to dry my hands after each shot.

I began the round amped up by my normal competitive adrenaline and made par on the first two holes but got into a little trouble on the third hole, a 440-yard par four. I played my tee shot into a twenty-five mile-per-hour gale force wind, and the rain was picking up. I hit the fairway but still had 200 yards to the green into a cold, wet breeze. I hit a hard four iron but hooked my ball twenty yards left of the green into thick, six-inch rough. The US Open is known for having very deep rough that is penalizing . . . and this qualifier was sticking to US Open tradition.

When I got to my ball, it was so buried in the bluegrass that I could only see the top third of the ball. I would have to hit a sky-high lob shot à la Phil Mickelson, over a green-side bunker to a hole that was cut only fifteen feet from the closest edge of the green. The only thing I could see was the grassy hill right in front of me—the shot was totally blind. I would have to rely on visualization to pull off the shot. I inspected the shot from the top of the hill and then went down to the base, where my brother was holding my bag and the umbrella, ready to discuss strategy.

"No need to be a hero this early in the round," he said. "It wouldn't be a bad play to get it fifteen feet past the hole and try and make a putt."

I pulled my sixty-degree lob wedge out of the bag, but I had no intention to take his advice to play safe. I took a big swing, as if to hit a really long shot and sliced underneath the ball with my wedge. The shot went straight up into the air and sailed over the top of the hill, just as I had imagined it. I couldn't see the ball land because of the slope, but my brother could. He had moved up next to the green to see where the ball would finish.

"Where is it?" I barked at him.

"It lipped out and stopped a foot from the hole," he explained, flashing me a thumbs-up signal.

It's a shot that I might pull off once in every twenty-five tries, but executing it in that moment was a huge confidence boost and set the tone for the entire round. When you pull off any gamble in golf, it frees you, relaxes you. I tapped in for par and eased into the rhythm of the round.

I made par on the fourth hole, a difficult 210-yard par three guarded by bunkers and a large pond. I made back-to-back birdies on the fifth and sixth holes before making par on number seven. I made a mistake on the eighth hole when I pulled my tee shot into a green-side bunker to make bogey, but I managed a par on number nine to end the front nine in one under par. My approach shot on the tenth hole came to rest eight feet from the hole, and I rolled in the birdie putt to get back to two under for the day. I ended the game with five consecutive pars.

Typically if a player finishes a round anywhere under par at the local qualifier in St. Louis, he has a good chance of advancing to the sectional qualifier. I had played in this event enough times to gauge what I needed to shoot in order to advance. At two under par approaching the sixteenth hole, I knew I had a very good chance to qualify.

The sixteenth hole at WingHaven is a twisting par five that played directly into the wind, and the rain was starting to really come down. I blocked my tee shot well to the right and was lucky that my ball landed in bounds. I hit a seven-iron lay-up shot down the fairway in order to set up a wedge for my approach, but I pulled the shot badly into the gnarly rough just left of the fairway. I had 145 yards to a shallow green that was guarded by a creek running across its entire front. For the first time that day, I needed reassurance from my brother.

"Kev, what if we just chop this ball down the fairway, short of the creek, and try and get it up and down from there and save par?" I asked him, feeling like I needed to take a conservative approach.

"The lie isn't that bad. You should be able to hit it on the green from here no problem," he replied, changing my mind.

I tried to punch an eight-iron shot, but the rough grabbed my club and forced the ball immediately left, and it came out dead and dove into the creek. Forced to take a penalty and drop my ball short of the creek water hazard, I hit an indifferent pitch to about ten feet, then missed the bogey putt and had to tap in for a costly double bogey. As soon as I tapped in, the air horn blew from the clubhouse, signaling a weather delay. As we walked from the sixteenth green to the clubhouse for shelter, I looked at my brother.

"What do you think about laying up to the creek and playing safe now?" I asked him.

"No way."

"Why not?"

"It wasn't that hard of a shot," he poked at me with a grin.

He was right. The weather delay gave me some time to cool off. When I was younger, my anger would sometimes take over when I hit a bad shot. Knowing what I know now about bipolar disorder, it is easy to see how anger clouded my mind on the golf course. Had I allowed the bipolar anger to take over at this point in the game, I would have lost my concentration. But, having become well, I was experiencing healthy anger and was thankful for the weather delay to allow me the time to wind down.

We waited about forty-five minutes for the rain to pass and went back to the seventeenth tee. I played a three wood to the fairway and a nine iron into the middle of the green to make a solid par. One hole left to play; I figured I needed a birdie.

The final hole at WingHaven is a sharp dogleg-left par four that plays severely uphill on the second shot. I played my customary left-to-right ball flight with my driver and found the middle of the fairway. The shot traveled only about 240 yards, stopping immediately when it hit the wet fairway. I still had 179 yards, but the shot would play closer to 190 yards with the adjustment of the slope up the hill. I chose my six iron and took aim at the flag on the right side of the green. But, I pulled the shot about thirty-five feet left of the hole.

I now had a tough play on my hands. I needed to strike hard to make the putt, but I couldn't be too aggressive and knock my birdie putt well past the hole. A birdie at eighteen would give me 71. I put a good roll on it, but it lost speed; the ball missed the cup just right of the hole and finished about two feet away. I finished play around 12:30 p.m. with a 72 and would have to wait until 5:30 p.m. or even 6:00 p.m. to find out if my score was good enough.

Eleven players had shot 72, including me. We would fight it out for seven spots in a sudden-death playoff, beginning at the tenth hole. My earlier birdie on that hole made me feel good about starting there.

The officials sent us in two groups; I was assigned to the first group of five. My adrenaline was pumping as I placed my ball on a black tee and I used it to obliterate the ball with my customary high fade. I found the right side of the fairway and had 125 yards left for my second shot. Two of the players in my fivesome played their second shots from the fairway before I did, and both of them hit their approach shots over the green. That was the worst place to land their balls because the hole, in the back middle of the putting surface, sits at the bottom of a valley; any shot from behind the green would be impossible to stop near the hole.

Normally, 125 yards would be a comfortable pitching-wedge shot for me, but I grabbed my fifty-six-degree sand wedge because the wind would help me out. The swing was perfect; it had that crisp *woosh* sound that all golfers yearn to hear. The ball left the clubface and seemed to hunt the flagstick, staying on line with its target until it came to earth twelve feet below the hole, giving me good opportunity to birdie.

I was nervous as I stood over my putt. The tendency when you are nervous is to leave putts short, and that's exactly what I did—the ball stopped two inches short of the hole, aligned dead center with the middle of the cup.

Two players in my fivesome had made bogey, and three of us made par on that first hole of the playoff. The sixsome behind us all made par as my group watched. The two players who had made bogey were eliminated at that hole, leaving nine players to play on for seven spots.

The next hole in the playoff was number eighteen because it ran adjacent to the tenth hole. I found the fairway with my tee shot and walked off the eighteenth tee grinning from ear to ear.

Because it was nearly sunset, and there wasn't enough time to play two groups, the officials combined us into a single group of nine—all accomplished pros or hotshot amateurs, as well as the best players in town. Five made par to earn spots. One player was eliminated. I made bogey, along with two others, and had to return to the tenth hole to play for the remaining two spots. But, with the sun going down, darkness seized the afternoon and made it difficult to play.

The three-man duel included Todd Meyer, Scott Moore, and me. Meyer, a seasoned pro, dominant player, and exceptional teacher in the Gateway PGA Section in the St. Louis area, had had made a run at the PGA Tour when he was younger. Moore had been a standout player at the University of Arizona and had recently turned pro to make his own run at the PGA Tour.

I had the honor to play first. As I stood over my tee shot and took one last look at my target, a golf cart raced across the fairway. I backed off. An official was trying to get to the left side of the fairway in case any of our tee shots landed on the left portion of the hole.

The official on the tenth tee immediately picked up his walkie-talkie. "Gentlemen, let's stay still out there; we are ready to play back here. Hold still! Sorry about that, Mr. Wellington. Please proceed."

"No sweat." I replied. I didn't let it bother me.

I stepped up to the ball again, but before I even had a chance to take my final look at the target, another cart made its way across the fairway. I backed off again. Officials are the only people allowed to use golf carts at USGA events, but it was clear that this idiot going back and forth in the fairway was not seasoned.

Now the official on the tenth tee was pissed off. "What the hell is going on out there?" he barked into his walkie-talkie. "Don't anyone move until we get to the green!"

I was pissed off, too, but tried to be patient and diffuse the situation.

"Do these people know this isn't a Tuesday night scramble in the local beer league?" I said to Moore and Meyer in disbelief. Meyer laughed.

I stepped to the tee for a third time and drove the ball into the right rough. Meyer and Moore both hit the fairway. I had 154 yards to the hole, but my ball was in the worst lie I had seen all day. I hacked out a nine-iron shot to about forty yards short of the green, but in the fairway. Meyer and Moore both hit the green with their second shots.

I was in serious trouble.

I had an awkward distance of thirty-seven yards to the hole and had to fly the ball over a sand trap that guarded the flagstick. My ball was sitting in soaking, muddy zoysia grass. It was basically dark outside, and the pressure of the playoff was intense. Even though this was a tough shot, I loved every part of the challenge. I played a decent pitch to fifteen feet left of the hole; I'd have to make the putt to save par. Moore two-putted for par, and Meyer did the same. It was up to me to push the playoff into the next day with a fifteen-footer and darkness setting in.

I made my read, stood over my ball, and let the putt go. The ball was tracking on line with the cup and narrowly missed grabbing the right edge of the hole as it slipped a few feet past my target. I shook hands with Moore first and told him congratulations.

Meyer then came over to shake hands and patted me on the back. "That was bullshit what happened back on the tee when you were trying to play."

"Maybe, but the guy in the cart didn't block my tee shot into the right rough; that was all me," I answered with a wry smile. My response came from the John Wooden philosophy: *Don't whine, don't complain, and don't make excuses.* The experience taught me to be prepared for anything and everything, a lesson for both golf and life.

* * *

After the playoff at WingHaven, I accomplished some good things on the golf course that summer. I shot 64 at the Iowa Open in Waterloo, Iowa, and also fired a round of 62 in a practice round at home at Westborough, which made me feel like I was headed in the right direction for Q-School.

I caddied and worked as a courier for my dad's printing company to earn the money to pay for Q-School. I was on a good path.

The first stage of Q-School was held at The Oaks Golf Club in Pass Christian, Mississippi. I had Johnny Mullin back on the bag. We had played a lot of golf together that summer, so he knew my game almost as well as I did, and he made sure I took my lithium each morning before we got to the golf course.

We made the eleven-hour drive from St. Louis to southern Mississippi. I started the tournament very focused and played my first two rounds in one under par, shooting 71 and 72. After thirty-six holes, I was tied for eighteenth place. The top nineteen finishers and ties would advance to the second stage. But I struggled with my nerves and my anger during the last two days and didn't advance with my scores of 74 and 75. Still, I got a small taste of being in the mix.

During my first trip to Q-School, I hadn't been focused enough at the start of the tournament, but I didn't have that issue this time around. To me, my showing was an improvement. I took time to reevaluate and make a new strategy for the following year, but in the meantime, I needed to make money.

* * *

I worked at a cabinetmaking company in November and December of 2003. My duties were to deliver heavy, handmade cabinets and large pieces of furniture all around the greater St. Louis area. I also swept floors in the warehouse. The job truly humbled me. After eight weeks of hard labor, I had made enough money to make the move to Las Vegas to continue working on my golf game over the winter. The always-windy conditions in Vegas would help my game; I would have to learn how to play low shots into the wind. Plus, Vegas would be fun!

I spent the first five months of 2004 in Las Vegas, working for a company that produced blue-lens eyeglasses that were marketed to senior golfers who had trouble finding golf balls in the rough. Mullin moved out there with me, and we found a house in a neighborhood at the south end of the strip. Many of our rent payments came from winnings on college and pro sports gambles.

I didn't have any bipolar issues the entire time that we lived there. I was religious about taking my medicine every morning, and it provided me a much-needed level of stability for living in a place like Sin City. Although I didn't have any problems with my disorder, I still allowed some old bad habits back into my life.

I began to drink again. I didn't have any blackout nights, but I was drinking regularly. Every other weekend, it seemed, groups of friends came to Vegas to party; I met up with all of them, and there were many nights when we saw the sun rise. Drinking and an inconsistent sleep schedule are a dangerous combination with bipolar disorder.

My golf swing improved. My swing had always been too long, and there was a small loop at the top of my backswing that probably came from trying to copy Fred Couples when I was a teenager. So I spent hours with a bungee cord wrapped around my arm while I hit practice balls at the driving range. I hit so many balls with that cord attached to my arm that I had friction wounds in the crook of my elbow. But, my swing got shorter and more consistent.

* * *

When I returned to St. Louis in the spring, I continued enjoying the night-life, juggling multiple women, drinking like a fish, and staying out all night. I got so comfortable at home in St. Louis that I completely disregarded my health—all of it—mental, physical, and emotional.

Common sense tells you that if something is working well, don't change it. The consistency and the healthy result of daily medication in Las Vegas should have convinced me to continue taking the medication when I moved home. But one of the issues with my bipolar mind is that when things are going well, my ego gets in the way; I started to believe I could handle my life without medication because I hadn't had depression or manic episodes in more than two years.

At twenty-six years old I thought I knew everything. In reality, I didn't know shit, especially about bipolar disorder. Many bipolar people with whom I have compared experiences also share stories about living a normal life while taking meds and then, for some reason, they stop taking their medicine and experience a wild episode. Bipolar disorder is sneaky like that. It's a lot like golf: Just when you think you have it licked, it will jump up and humble you. With bipolar disease, manic episodes are around every corner, but it has taken me years to realize that.

* * *

Fox Run Golf Club, in Eureka, Missouri, held the 2004 US Open local qualifier. The day was awful from start to finish. Afterward, in the parking lot, I had a meltdown. I violently chucked my golf shoes into the trunk and slammed my trunk closed when my dad, who had come out to watch the end of my round, pulled up to my car.

"I am working my ass off and I can't break through," I complained to him.

"It takes time," he said consolingly. "If you want to do this, you have to be able to handle the bad days too. Not every day in golf is going to be a great day. Golf doesn't work like that."

The day after that qualifier, I went off my medicine. All golfers—all athletes—constantly try to get better and will do just about anything to help that along; I was no different. I justified dropping my meds by thinking it might improve my golf. I also bought all new equipment, spending money I couldn't afford to waste. My thirst to improve was conspiring against me.

The summer of 2004 wasn't very good for me on the golf course, mostly because of drinking and late-night partying, but I had one amazing round while at a reunion with some of my college friends in Destin, Florida. I shot 65 at Kelly Plantation; that round changed my mind about going to Q-School in the fall. I was going.

The first stage of Q-School was at Martin Downs Country Club in Palm City, Florida, a regular site for the first stage of Q-School. It is a very fair and flat course where the wind howls, making it a perfect test.

I didn't have a caddie when I got to Martin Downs for my practice rounds but, as I walked through the parking area to the driving range, I met Tony T. He wore his North Carolina hat up high on his forehead, two gold chains on his right wrist, and another around his neck—they were clearly visible because none of the buttons on his golf shirt were secured. He smiled as he told me that he used to caddie for Duffy Waldorf and Vijay Singh. I hired him as soon as I heard Vijay's name. Singh was the number-one-ranked player in the world at the time.

Tony T grabbed my bag and off we went to the first tee for a practice round. He taught me a few short-game shots that Vijay had showed him. I learned a lot from him that week, but I scored terribly. Every morning, before each tournament round, I was as nervous as I usually was before a competitive round at Q-School. But mentally I was all over the place; my bipolar disorder was slowly creeping back into my life.

One morning before my first round, I was feeling paranoid as I pulled my clubs out of the trunk so I got back into the car and took 900 milligrams of lithium (my regular daily dose was 1,200) to try and calm myself. It was classic self-medication and especially dangerous because I hadn't taken my medicine in months.

I blamed my poor performance in the first round that day on taking the meds, so I didn't take any before my second round. I played even worse. On the morning of the third round, I remember taking a single 300-milligram pill, grabbing my clubs from the trunk, putting on my golf shoes, and then taking two more pills. In my mind, I had played better with the three pills in my system, like the first round when I had taken 900 milligrams, than I had with no lithium in my system during the second round. While I knew that a single day's dose would not directly affect my golf game, bipolar disorder had taken away any ability to think clearly in that moment.

On the fourth and final day of practice rounds, I decided to split the difference of the previous days' doses and take just two pills. The intensity of Q-School and my instability for months on end without medication had turned me into a superstitious junkie searching for a quick fix every morning in the parking lot. I was embarrassed about my play and regretted my decision to enter Q-School. I had posted rounds of 77–76–78–77 to miss qualifying by ten miles.

* * *

I headed back to St. Louis to face my dad, who had helped pay the $4,000 entry fee for Q-School. It was the first time I was certain my dad would challenge me about my decision to play professional golf. I could feel it coming.

Because my dad had played a lot of tournament golf, he understood the game well. So, after each of my tournament rounds, I would usually call him to dissect the game with me. It was a tradition that we started when I played in college and we still continue to this day. My dad has always been positive with me about my play, always encouraging. He never got on me about missing a putt or shooting a bad score. He didn't push me to play; he allowed me to fall in love with the game on my own, and he had watched my talent grow as I worked hard through the years.

He didn't answer my call after the final round.

My parents were getting ready for Sunday night dinner when I arrived at their house. The tournament had ended on Friday, and I had driven more than ten hours a day to make it back by Sunday night. I wasn't in the house five minutes when my dad let me have it.

"What were you doing down there? Those were bad rounds."

"What can I say, Dad? I played badly," I said. "Sometimes that happens."

He scolded me. "You need to start thinking about doing something else if you are going to play rounds like that in your third crack at that tournament. You weren't even close, and you haven't gotten any better."

For the first time, my dad was critical about my golf career, and it killed me. He had always been my number-one supporter. He supported me when no one else did. My mom didn't say a word while my dad and I volleyed back and forth. It became ugly, and I stormed out of the house.

"I will eat somewhere else. I can't handle you, Dad."

"See if they serve a dose of reality wherever you decide to eat tonight!" He yelled as I walked through the kitchen door.

I headed to a place where I knew I would be welcome. Three of my good friends from high school—Ryan Schuette, Ryan Weber, and Matt Ratz—had just moved into a house in the western suburbs of St. Louis. When I told them I was staying in St. Louis for the winter, they offered to rent me a room. These were good friends and good people. Matt Ratz is a champion of life; he donated his kidney to his younger sister.

In retrospect, my dad was exactly right. I needed a dose of reality. I had been drinking too much, chasing too many women, and had gone off my medication. First and foremost, I needed to take my lithium every day. But I was twenty-six and thought I knew everything. I began another self-destructive climb up a brand new manic ladder. The monster was lurking and wanted me badly, and I couldn't fight it. I stepped away from professional golf for the winter of 2005 and ran willingly into the direction of my demons.

THE FOURTEEN CLUBS

I was healthy and symptom free for the first half of 2004 because I had maintained a constant routine and consistent daily medication, albeit clouded by too much drinking. My troubles began again in earnest when I started messing with the formula: when I stopped taking my lithium and started self-medicating.

4

THE DISASTER AT FOREST HILLS

Victory belongs to the most persevering.
—*Napoleon Bonaparte*

IT HAD BEEN nine months since I last took my medication, but I had hidden it from those around me. I was living with my buddies, drinking, gambling, and chasing women. I wasn't sleeping. I didn't need sleep, not when the bars and gentlemen's clubs were open until all hours of the morning and I had an excess of manic energy. My disorder overtook any rational thoughts to stay home and rest.

My evenings began at Harpo's, my favorite sports bar in the western suburbs of St. Louis. There I would have two Coronas, two 7 and 7s, and a random shot—my pregame drinks. I would leave Harpo's around nine o'clock and head east down Highway 40 with a light buzz. It was common for me to drink and drive; I continued that terrifying practice for many years before shaking the booze.

I always made my second stop in Clayton, an area with a dozen or so bars to choose from. I'd hop from bar to bar enjoying Crown and Coke, Bud Light, 7 and 7, Sapporo, Jägermeister, and Busch. There was never any consistency to what I drank. I mixed it up and didn't keep track.

Near midnight, after carousing around Clayton for a few hours, it was time to head downtown to Washington Street. I'd have a solid three hours until the bars closed, after which I'd make the ten-minute jaunt east across the Mississippi River to the strip clubs in Southern Illinois. The gentlemen's clubs in Illinois are well known around the St. Louis area, and they never close. There were many mornings that I was blinded by the sun as I exited a club at 6:00 or 7:00 a.m. I was enjoying a bottomless pit of booze and strippers and never tired of it—my manic energy ran the show.

The absence of medication in my system had allowed my old manic behavior to surface. I would talk so fast that my words jumbled together. I raced from bar to bar with an alarming sense of urgency. I couldn't sit still. But I was blind to the telltale symptoms of mania. When a person is in the grips of mania, their awareness is taken from them. Bipolar mania can be obvious to everyone except the person who has the disorder. When alcohol is added to the mix, anything can happen. And it's rarely, if ever, anything good.

In spite of my drinking binges, I chose to begin preparing for the US Open qualifier in early May 2005 at Forest Hills Country Club in west-suburban St. Louis. It would be my first competitive round of the year.

The day before the qualifier, I went out to Forest Hills for a practice round in full manic mode. I felt energized and light on my feet, oblivious that manic excitement was overshadowing the familiar enemy that was lurking just around the corner.

After leaving the practice session, around 3:30, I headed straight to The Country Club, a bar close to the course. The place was empty except for the bartender and a few patrons, all in business attire. As I sat on the barstool, I couldn't stop tapping my feet on the spot where the bar met the floor. I noticed a man in his fifties wearing a black suit sitting two stools down and staring right at me.

"You getting ready to go to dance class?" he asked with a sly smirk.

I looked right through him, not responding. When I am manic, I tend to act as if everyone around me is either invisible or the deserving recipient of rude comments. But something held me back in that moment. His eyes were blood shot and he had a sheepish grin, which told me he had been on that barstool for a long time.

The bartender put a beer in front of me. I guzzled it without taking a breath, demonstrating another of my manic symptoms: Everything is a race—even to finish a drink. I also become so restless that I can't stay in one place for long. The sense of urgency inside my manic mind becomes relentless.

After slamming down my empty bottle, I threw down more than enough money for the beer and a tip, made a beeline for my car, and drove away. I was there no more than ten minutes.

I drove to another bar closer to my house and did the exact same thing with a shot of Wild Turkey and a 7 and 7. I slapped down thirty bucks and was out in five minutes.

The strippers in east St. Louis were the obvious next stop for me, as the mania elevated my sex drive. I headed to the clubs in Sauget as the sun was setting. I sat on a couch away from the stage with my baseball cap pulled down low over my eyes. I must have looked like the stereotypical creep. But, again, I didn't stay very long—only about fifteen minutes.

When I walked out of the club, I called my old pal Matt Rebstock and asked him if I could stay at his house that night. He was curious why I would want to sleep on a couch the night before an important tournament round, but he didn't refuse. I got to his place around eleven o'clock, and we watched a movie in his living room. I was finally able to relax. The film was *Man On Fire*, starring Denzel Washington—how ironic that I was finally calm while watching a movie with that title.

Rebstock went to bed when the film ended and I made an unsuccessful attempt to sleep on his couch, my feet hanging off the side of the couch. The anticipation of the qualifier, plus my increasing mania, kept me awake all night. I vividly remember looking at the clock every other minute as I tossed and turned. I left Rebstock's place at 5:30 the next morning.

* * *

My tee time was 7:48. I was to meet my caddie David Pfyl, who was a childhood friend with whom I had played junior and high school golf, in the parking lot at Westborough at 6:10. The plan was to drive to Forest Hills and golf. We agreed to meet at the park.

When David arrived at Westborough, he found my green Honda parked next to the practice green, the trunk open and all the windows down, rap music blaring. I danced in between each practice putt that I hit. David approached me, and we shook hands. He watched my odd and quick behavior for a few minutes but didn't say anything. He finally began asking questions.

"Did you do a bunch of coke on your way here?"

"No," I laughed at his question and continued to dance on the green, hitting practice putts. Cocaine had never been my drug, mostly because Celtics first-round draft pick Len Bias lost his life to a cocaine overdose in the mid-1980s and it scared me away from ever using it.

"Did you take ecstasy? Were you up all night?" I had tried ecstasy in college, but it had been years since I had had any.

"No, I'm totally sober."

"Well, why are you wearing your dress shoes?"

I looked down at myself. I was very particular about my tournament golf attire: I would never wear the same color trousers and shirt, and I always wore long dark socks for a tournament. On this morning, I was wearing white pants and a white shirt and tuxedo shoes with no socks.

I raced from the green to my car, put the putter back in my golf bag, and slammed the trunk. "David, we gotta get going. I'll drive. Let's go! Let's go! But we have to make one stop on the way." David hopped in and I drove.

We stopped at St. Joseph's Church in the western suburbs, about ten minutes from Forest Hills. I was raised with a strong faith, and when I slip into mania my mind often focuses on religion, imagining that I am caught in a battle between good and evil: God versus Satan, heaven versus hell, or the living versus the dead. In the grip of mania, I often made my way to a church to feel safe from the imaginary evil that seemed to hunt me. Or, it could also be that I saw *The Exorcist* way too early in life. It. Freaked. Me. Out.

When David and I pulled into the parking lot at St. Joseph's, there was chaos—it was car pool drop-off.

"What the fuck are we doing here?" David never beat around the bush.

"Just stay here. I'll be right back."

I hopped out of the car while it was still running and weaved my way through the minivans in my all-white attire and my ball cap on backward. I approached the life-size statue of St. Joseph perched atop the small fountain near the church entrance. His arms were extended outward, with his palms facing up toward the sky. Dozens of soccer moms—and David—watched me race up to the statue and slap St. Joseph a high-five, then turn around and sprint back to my car.

"What did you just do?"

"I just gave St. Joseph five for good luck."

I felt safe. I could breathe again. And I could play the course ahead of me.

* * *

There was a lot of traffic that morning, and the detour to the church put us behind schedule. We pulled into the parking lot at Forest Hills fifteen minutes before my tee time. Once we parked, I switched into my golf shoes but didn't put on any socks. David grabbed the bag, and we headed immediately to the tee box.

We were paired with Paul Neeman, who is a very nice man and a very good player. He played events on the old Nike Tour, which would be equivalent to today's Web.com Tour. Terry Yake, a former St. Louis Blues hockey player and fine golfer, was the third player in our group.

I would start on the tenth hole, a 345-yard, downhill, dogleg-right par four that plays more like 315 yards because of the downhill factor. If I hit a good driver with my customary fade, I could easily reach the green with my tee shot. David and I decided to be conservative, so I played a six iron to the left side of the fairway to set up a full wedge shot onto the green.

I wasn't nervous at all on my opening tee shot, and that was a bad sign. Most tournament golfers will tell you that there are always nerves on the first tee; feeling uneasy on the first tee is a good thing, normal. I was so exhausted that I didn't feel anything. I hit the fairway with a six-iron shot, and that was the only positive in the whole round. I missed the green with my wedge and ended up in a green-side bunker with my ball buried in the sand. I bogeyed the hole and followed it with a blizzard of poor play, bad course management, an embarrassing lack of proper etiquette, and a nightmare finish.

My behavior was ridiculously out of character for me throughout the day. After I played my tee shots, I race-walked to my second shots, leaving my entire group—and David, my bagman—behind.

A player never leaves his caddie's side during a competitive round; the caddie is the only teammate a golfer has. At the end of the day, a good caddie can make a world of difference, and a good golfer knows this. One of my personal favorite aspects of tournament golf is the banter back and forth between a player and his caddie. David is an extremely witty and funny guy, but I was on a different planet that day.

I followed my opening bogey with a double bogey on my second hole and finally made par on my third hole. I was in such a hurry to play each shot that I was literally panting as I made my way down the fairway to my fourth hole—another bogey. I managed to make par on the next two holes.

On the seventh hole, I noticed my parents were in the gallery, watching my round. My parents very rarely watched me play; it made my mom very nervous and my dad usually didn't have the free time. Two days before the qualifier I called my mom specifically to ask her to come out to Forest Hills to watch. I had never done that before—another out of character move. Even though the mania had taken over and I was locked into tournament golf concentration mode, I walked over and kissed my mom hello.

There is a steep walk up a flight of railroad-tie stairs to get to the tee box at par-three hole sixteen, my seventh hole in that round. I distinctly remember becoming aware that a battle between good and evil was raging as I approached the stairs. I felt like I had to hunt the evil at all costs. About three steps from the top, I saw a small ladybug clinging to my right shoelace.

Satan has taken the form of this ladybug, I warned myself. *Where can I put it so it can't hurt anyone else? I have to trap it, because if I kill it, it may come back to life. I can swallow it. It will never be able to escape my belly, because I never throw up. My stomach is a steel trap.*

I grabbed the ladybug off the laces and put it in my mouth, then chased it down my throat with a sip of water. No one in my group saw this because my speed walking had put me far in front of everyone else. I actually felt good about swallowing the ladybug, because, in my mind, I was helping others. It is another of the inexplicable, interesting, odd, and dangerous things that bipolar disorder does to the mind: The mania constructs far-fetched fantasies and makes them seem perfectly normal.

At some point, my etiquette on course became an issue. I began whistling loudly as I walked down the fairways between shots. I would also whistle immediately after any of my playing partners made their shots. In golf, a quiet game of tradition and manners, my behavior was bordering on inappropriate.

On the eighteenth tee, my ninth hole of the day, I played first and finally hit a solid shot into the middle of the fairway. As my ball came to rest, I walked back to my bag, gave the three-wood club to David, and looked at my playing partners.

"Chase that," I challenged.

Now I was trash-talking. I was always taught to respect the game of golf, to respect the rules, and to respect the people who play the game. In golf, integrity is essential. In other sports, you are competing against your opponents; in golf, you are competing against the golf course, and you let your clubs do your talking for you. It's the only game in the world in which a player can call a penalty on himself.

Research shows that bipolar disorder is a shame-based disorder. Does a person develop it because he is ashamed of an aspect of his life—the shame triggering a chemical imbalance? Or is the shame created as a result of having the disorder? Or is it both? Either way, I often felt ashamed, defective. It's easy to see why; I ate a ladybug because I thought it was the devil—there's nothing normal about that. Plus, when I look back on the day at Forest Hills, I feel—and remember feeling at the time—ashamed. My actions toward the players in my group were absolutely deplorable. With a clear and medicated mind, I never would have behaved that way. Bipolar disorder has the frightening ability to turn a person into someone else, someone who has little regard for his or her surroundings and who is enduring a mental tornado of erratic thoughts.

I know there is nothing defective about me, and there wasn't at the time. But it's the battle of the disorder—not to become convinced that you are defective. But when I chose to stop taking my medicine, to drink too much, to throw money around, and to regularly visit strip clubs, I allowed the storm of mania to brew within until it became torrential. To outsiders, who couldn't know what I was battling, I looked like an arrogant nut.

On my fourteenth hole of the day, I accused David of putting my bag down inside a water hazard line and tried to call a two-stroke penalty on myself. In reality, he had not put the bag anywhere near the hazard, but it didn't matter one way or the other. At ten over par, I didn't have a prayer of qualifying at that point anyway. That's right, ten over par.

When David and I finally reached hole nine, the last hole of the round, I was a complete mess. The ninth hole at Forest Hills is a par five with a sharp dogleg to the right that plays severely uphill on the third shot. I snap-hooked my tee shot into the tall trees immediately to the left of the teeing ground. The ball didn't travel more than eighty yards and never rose higher than fifteen feet off the ground. The ball was lost, and I had to re-tee. It was probably the worst shot that I have ever played in a competition—ugly, ugly, ugly.

I finally got my ball onto the green about twenty feet from the hole, but I was petrified as I stood there. Visions of planes crashing into the World Trade Center had begun to race through my mind. I just knew that as soon as any of the players in our group made a putt, the world would blow up. *Kaboom!* I didn't want to see any balls disappear into the hole. I kept removing my cap from my head and putting it back on feverishly. All the while, I tried to maintain my poker face.

Yake's putt made it into the hole to finish his round. The horror within me began building. Then Neeman putted a twenty-five-footer for a birdie from the fringe of the green. I was scared to death that because nothing bad had happened when Yake's ball went in, Neeman's ball would start a horrible chain reaction. So, I whispered the classic taunting line from *Caddyshack*. "Miss it . . . mmmmiss it . . . mmmmiss it!"

My choice to verbally assault Neeman was opposed to everything I had ever learned about respecting other players. But my demonic pride raged. My integrity was siphoned into oblivion—perhaps by the ladybug rolling around in my stomach.

Neeman backed off his putt and, with good reason, looked at me as if I had seven heads. I walked toward him with my right arm extended and my hand out, offering him a handshake. David grabbed me by the collar and stopped me.

"Leave the guy alone and let him putt, or I am going to beat the hell out of you right here on the green," he whispered in my ear.

Neeman got back over his putt and missed it. *Whew, the world isn't ending yet,* I reassured myself. But then he tapped it in. I looked around. Everyone was still in one piece; the breeze blew, and the trees swayed.

I was up. I looked at my twenty-footer, and hit the ball to a foot short of the hole. As I stood over the easy one-foot putt, my mind was racked with the fear that if the putt dropped, all mankind would perish.

What to do? Just miss it on purpose.

So, I overshot the hole by three feet.

And now what? Miss it again. That ball CANNOT go into the hole.

I took a one-handed polo swipe at the ball and knocked it clear off the green, down a steep slope, fifty yards away. David went and picked up my ball at the bottom of the hill; I was disqualified for not finishing the final hole.

I need to get out of here. I need to get to my car.

We walked to the scoring area. As I sat down the exhaustion enveloped my body as if it were a disease. I was sweating, restless, twitching, and paranoid. Fear engulfed me. One of the rules officials told me that I would have to sign Neeman's card to make the round official for him.

I rebuked him. "I'm not signing anything," I told the official.

I was so confused and paranoid that I was afraid to simply sign the scorecard. I must have uttered something out loud, because the USGA rules official, Tom O'Toole, came to the scoring tent and assured me nothing bad would happen if I signed the card. O'Toole and my dad grew up playing golf together, and he was a close family friend. He was aware of my bipolar issues—he had seen some of my bipolar behavior in Fort Myers back in 2001—and could clearly see that something was not right. O'Toole assured me that it would be okay for me to sign the scorecard, and because of my trust in him, I finally signed it.

After signing the card, I walked back to the parking lot to find David standing at my car with my clubs. At this point in our friendship, he had no idea that I had bipolar disorder. I couldn't tell him in that moment because my awareness level of what was happening to me was nonexistent. I didn't even know that what I had done was wrong or that I was in the middle of a serious episode.

Where the fuck am I, and what have I done?

* * *

I left Maroon Creek after the summer of 2000. This wasn't the first time I had exhibited inappropriate behavior on the course, but I wasn't aware of a pattern at the time. The day before I left Maroon Creek, where I had met Tiger Woods, I ran into Tom Hoffmaster, an old friend, on the driving range. I wanted to thank him for everything he had done for me over the last two seasons. I had caddied for him for two straight summers, and he had always treated me and my fellow caddies like sons. I looked up to him.

The conversation started out pleasantly but quickly turned. "Ya know,

Mikey, you need to get your shit together! You need to lose the attitude and quit being so cocky and arrogant all the time."

I just listened; he wasn't a guy I wanted to argue with.

"You hear what I am telling you, kid? You have a lot of personality and you're a great golfer, but you have to learn how to treat people better and learn when to talk and when to keep your mouth shut!" He was hot; I'd never seen this side of him. I hadn't realized I'd been acting like an ass, but when he said it, I knew he was right. I almost burst into tears right in front of him, but I kept it together.

"You're right, Hoffy. I need to work on all of it. I came down here to tell you thanks for everything, because I'm leaving tomorrow."

"Alright, kid. Good luck, and keep in touch."

When I walked away from him, tears welled up in my eyes. The coolest man I have ever met had just lit me up like a Christmas tree. After growing up a little, I realized that he had done it for my own good, to help knock some sense into me. At the time, his words rocked my world, but bipolar disorder can blind you to your behavior, even after someone you respect has directly pointed it out.

I didn't realize how I had acted to David and Neeman and Yake at the Forest Hills qualifier until about a month later, after a pair of hospital stays and resuming my medication. I wrote apology letters to both Neeman and Yake, telling them about my bipolar disorder and how embarrassed I was that it had caused such anarchy during our round together.

* * *

David drove my car back to Westborough; he didn't feel comfortable allowing me behind the wheel after what had transpired on the golf course. We spent most of the drive in silence. Years later, David admitted to me that he was spooked by my actions at Forest Hills. Even though he had known me for twenty years, he said, he didn't know how to handle the situation. I had no idea he had wanted to rip my head off that day—I couldn't even tell that he was upset with me. Bipolar disorder blinds you to how you affect others.

In fact, I felt safe as we drove back to Westborough because I was with someone I trusted. After dropping David off at his car, that feeling of safety disappeared, quickly replaced by the conflict of good and evil once more.

Someone is trying to kill me. And it's Osama bin Laden.

I made a beeline for the safest place I could think of—the Missouri Athletic Club, in downtown St. Louis. I had spent a lot of time there; it was my health club, a place where I could stay if I had had too much to drink and didn't want to drive home drunk, and a place where I had attended many wedding receptions and parties over the years. I felt like it was a fortress where I could hide from bin Laden, at that time the world's most wanted, hated, and despised man. In my mind—and probably in the mind of many Americans—he was the devil incarnate.

When I arrived at the club, I went straight to the elevator banks. When the doors opened, I entered. A man in his midforties wearing a gray pinstripe suit and carrying a briefcase was already in the elevator. I just knew he was going to do something bad to me. I came close to punching him for no reason at all. Somehow, I managed to restrain myself and got off on the fifth floor. I walked directly into the locker room where I began to feel even more paranoid. I grabbed my cell phone and called my friend Nick Sansone, whom I have known since the sixth grade. Sansone is as loyal as they come and is very familiar with my battles with bipolar disorder. He had been at the airport with my mom and my younger brother when I returned to St. Louis from Florida in 2001.

"Nick, I think Osama bin Laden is trying to kill me," I said to his voice mail.

I made my way to the pool, swam a few laps, then got out and lay on the pool deck, exhausted. My heartbeat was so elevated that I couldn't be still, but I was too tired to get to my feet and walk around. I stayed on my back, trying to catch my breath and relax. I remember lying there, water dripping and my chest heaving violently with every breath, shivering because the pool deck was cold. I began to pray silently, feeling like I had no control over my body or my breathing.

I am dying.

The next thing I knew, my dad was standing over me. He helped me up and took me into the locker room where I sat on a bench with my head in my hands.

"Dad, Osama bin Laden is coming after me, and he is going to kill me."

"He isn't going to find you. Hop in the shower, Michael, and then we will go grab something to eat," he humored and reassured me.

My dad took me to his and my mother's house, where I stayed for several nights. My parents told me that, at the time, they felt able to deal with my disorder without a doctor's help because of the success that they had when I first came home from Florida.

But this time I was uncontrollable.

I didn't sleep for the next few nights. I would dribble a basketball in the kitchen, the basketball making a loud and annoying thud . . . thud . . . thud as it bounced on the linoleum. I'd dribble until my mom came downstairs to stop me. But, just as she would climb back into bed, I'd start up again. I would do restless push-ups and sit-ups for twenty minutes in the basement at three in the morning, then walk up the stairs to my parents' room and stand over my mom while she slept. I would stand there until she woke up to see me watching her. I would go to my childhood bedroom for five minutes or so, squirm around in my twin bed, and then head back down to the basement and turn the television on so loud that my dad would march down the stairs.

During the daytime, my behavior was completely outlandish. One day, I grabbed a Ben Hogan one iron out of the garage and began pacing up and down the street with it, like a parade marshal. Thank goodness it was a cul-de-sac.

My paranoia and aggression grew. *Someone is going to come and get me and torture me; I just know it. They're either going to come up from out of the ground or fall from the sky.* I was convinced it would be a fight to the death. I slammed the one iron into the pavement and challenged this imaginary killer to show himself.

"Come get me, motherfucker," I said under my breath as I paced up and down the street while alternately slamming the club into the asphalt and shaking it at the sky. "I am ready for you, you son of a bitch!" My voice began to grow louder with rage.

After banging my one iron until it was bent and scraped beyond repair, I chucked the club helicopter style into the garage and stormed inside. I could see the fear and concern on my mom's face when I walked into the kitchen. Just a few minutes later, my dad burst through the door. He got in my face, standing on his tiptoes.

"You need to get ahold of yourself! And no more drinking!" My dad is a recovering alcoholic who hadn't had a drink in twenty years.

I grabbed him, picked him up, and tossed him into the pantry closet. He tried to come back at me, but my size advantage kept him at bay, and I pushed him around the kitchen like a bully. My mom retreated upstairs and called the police.

Eventually, the fight moved outside onto the driveway, and that's where we were when the police showed up, followed close behind by an ambulance. The police were able to coerce me into getting into the back of the ambulance. Deep down I must have known I needed help, so I didn't argue.

My mixed bag of emotions contained anger at my parents for calling the authorities on me, curiosity about what lay ahead on my way to a hospital, and the feeling of relative safety with two friendly paramedics in the back of the ambulance. Most of the ride was quiet.

When I looked out the small square window in the rear door in the ambulance, I saw my parents following the ambulance in my dad's navy blue Jeep Cherokee. I was in my late twenties and felt like an infant. It was like my parents were pushing my stroller to the hospital.

The paramedics walked me inside the emergency entrance of St. Mary's Hospital—no stretcher or restraints this time. They put me in a room with an examination table. Within twenty minutes of my parents' arrival, my disdain for them vanished, and I was back to treating them with normal friendliness and respect. It was classic bipolar behavior—within twenty-five minutes I had gone from manhandling my dad to being calm and polite again.

Three hours passed. I couldn't sit still. I lay on the exam table, then sat Indian-style on the floor, then did push-ups in the small space of the floor, then started the cycle all over again. I was going in circles both mentally and physically.

My parents waited with me in the little box of an exam room. After three hours of no help from anyone, my dad left the room to hunt for a doctor or a nurse. Eventually, a young doctor wearing glasses and a Hawaiian shirt under his lab coat came in. He told bad jokes, but we had been in that room so long that no jokes would have entertained any of us at that point.

He quickly diagnosed me: textbook manic episode. He located the orderlies while I sat in a wheelchair in a blue hospital gown. I was wheeled off to the treatment floor—the psych ward—gripped by fear, engulfed by panic, and almost destroyed by paranoia.

I was scared to open my eyes as the elevator doors opened to deafening silence on the treatment floor. When I finally opened my eyes, I saw a woman in her fifties with silver hair quietly watching *The Oprah Winfrey Show* in an expansive sitting area with two large couches and three comfortable-looking chairs. The scene was almost relaxing. I felt relieved to be there after the torture of the small confines in the emergency room.

A long hallway stretched ahead of me with bright white floors and at least fifteen open doors on either wall. To my right was a nurse's desk with a few doctors and nurses milling around. I appreciated the quiet; it eased my mind and soothed that part of my memory that recalled the disorganized chaos of the Sarasota hospital.

Could a psych ward really be this serene?

A nurse led me to my room after I finished filling out paperwork; it was a single—no roommate—with a twin bed and a window looking out over Clayton Road, one of the busiest streets in St. Louis. The large bathroom had a shower, a toilet, and a sink.

This hospital stay was classified as "involuntary" because I had been brought in against my will. They could only keep me for seventy-two hours. At the time, I had no idea there was a difference between a voluntary and an involuntary stay. A patient admitted voluntarily has the option to stay inside the hospital until the doctors feel that the patient is completely stable and capable of resuming daily life. I have never had a voluntary stay inside a mental health facility.

* * *

Many people came to visit me during my three-day stay at St. Mary's. My cousin Shannon, a nurse at the hospital was the first to offer support. She assured me that I would get back to my normal life in a few days. It was reassuring to have her professional help and guidance in an uncertain situation.

"Mikey"—she has always called me Mikey—"all you need to do is listen to the doctors and nurses and you will be out of here before you know it."

Shannon, who had earned a field hockey scholarship to the University of Richmond, had been a great athlete herself and understood that I needed coaching. She played that role perfectly. I have always been coachable, so I listened: This was no time to panic; I should use this time to get well.

On the second morning at St. Mary's, I walked out of my room and stumbled into a ladder. As I steadied it, I noticed the shiny black loafers worn by the man working on the ceiling wiring. It was my uncle Thom.

"Thom! What the hell are you doing here?" I was so surprised to see him. Thom is an environmental engineer who owns his own company and, until this point, I had no idea he made house calls.

"Michael! We are doing some work on the building." He climbed down the ladder and gave me a big hug. He always had a smile on his face, just like his father had taught him.

"Did you know I was here?"

"No, is everything okay?"

I told him about my bipolar issues and that I was working on them.

Next up were my mom and my friend Matt Rebstock. Their visit had some twists and turns. Rebstock did most of the talking, speaking to me as if I were a two-year-old. It has not been uncommon in my experience that visitors in hospitals speak to patients like they're infants. I believe they think that, because you are sick, they need to change their inflection and tone in order to communicate with you. Rebstock and I have always had a conversational chemistry that flows like a river, and this was the first time that we struggled to talk to each other.

I was just about to tell him to quit the baby talk when a razor sharp pain gripped the right side of my neck. The pain shot from my neck into my mouth, and my tongue felt as if it had swollen to the size of a beach ball. My speech became so impaired that I spit out complete gibberish. I fell to my knees, screaming in pain from what felt like an enormous cramp that twisted my neck to the right. My mom rushed over to see what was happening. Rebstock put a hand on my shoulder and tapped me comfortingly. But I became angry that, in a matter of seconds, I had gone from being totally fine to writhing in pain. Nurses gave me a shot to release the cramping, but they had to put me back in my room immediately. I didn't get to finish talking with Rebstock and never got to speak with my mom.

It took about forty-five minutes for the discomfort to subside. It was an allergic reaction to some of the medication they were giving me. The drugs in psych wards are potent and often mixed with other medications into "cocktails"; bad reactions are common and can be painful and exhausting.

I remember counting the seconds, minutes, and hours on the clock on the wall as I lay in my room. It was so beautiful outside that the itch to play golf resurfaced, needing to be scratched.

And then in walked Dan Finney and Joan E. Steuby, dear friends of mine who had just started to date. I had known Dan since kindergarten. We had played soccer and baseball together for years, and he was familiar with the trials of bipolar disorder. He had been diagnosed in 2002, and I had helped him deal with some of the problems he had faced. I smiled at Dan from across the room as if to say, *Look at this. How'm I doing?* to which he shot back a look that said everything. It was his turn to return the favor.

Joan and I had met in high school. She had dated friends of mine, and I had dated friends of hers, but nothing romantic ever developed between us. Our friendship was—and still is—based on the tried-and-true foundation where iron sharpens iron. When I need to be called out on something, she'll show up, and I do the same for her.

Coincidentally, I had visited her in the very same hospital, when she was being treated for a dangerous case of spinal meningitis in 2003. She was in a coma when I saw her, connected to half a dozen machines that were keeping her alive. A clear plastic sheet separated her from anyone else in the room to keep her germ free. The only sounds in her room were a loud beep every few seconds paired with the contraction of a ventilator that sounded like Darth Vader. Her recovery was nothing short of a miracle.

Dan and Joan didn't stay very long, but it was long enough to help me feel grounded again. Joanie mentioned that my circumstances were a gift. Then, right before they left, she gave me a note:

5/18/2005

Wells,

I am so glad that you have given me the opportunity
to visit you at St. Mary's! Life is amazing, huh? You never
know what will be around the corner or what life will
hand you next. I believe that these challenges, Mike, are
really gifts—gifts that are given to us to challenge us in
ways we could never imagine. In some ways, I realize
how it seems to hinder us, but as long as we step up to
the plate and learn to take care of ourselves, it will make
us stronger individuals. Mike, this world has so much
to learn from you. You owe it to yourself and your loved
ones to take care of you, day in and day out. God would
not have dealt you these challenges if He did not feel you
could handle them. You are an amazing person, Michael!
I consider myself so blessed that I can call you a friend.
Know that I am always here for you in any way I can be.

Much Love,
Joan E.

I keep this note as a bookmark in a special journal that is always near
me. I look at it often to remind myself where my journey has taken me. But
it took me five or six years after she gave it to me to fully understand what
it meant. I am so proud to know Joan and have her as a member of my
circle of friends. She is an inspiration and an example of never giving up.

Dan also left me with a gift that afternoon: He told me about his doctor,
C. Robert Cloninger, with whom he had been working for a while. At the
time, I indulged Dan and told him I was interested but dismissed the idea
to myself. I still believed that I didn't need a shrink or medication; to me,
working with a psychiatrist was a sign of weakness.

What can I say? I was young and dumb. Seeking professional help
would have been the best thing I could do for myself.

By the time I was released from St. Mary's the doctors had gotten me back on my lithium and I promised to take it—just like I had promised in the past. Lies, lies, lies. I was just telling them what they wanted to hear so that I could get out of the hospital, to be on my own without doctors and nurses forcing pills down my throat every day.

My closest friends knew I had been in the hospital, but I had hidden it from most others. I had even hidden it from the great girl I was dating at the time, Kate. I worried that if she knew I was in the hospital, she wouldn't want to see me anymore. Shame reared its ugly head and began to sprout tentacles.

But Kate found out through the friend grapevine that I was in the hospital. St. Louis is a small town and news travels fast. Despite my fear, she didn't give up on me, even though she knew what I was going through. Kate stayed with me, but so did my ego and rebellious spirit. I quit taking the lithium as soon as I got out of St. Mary's; I tossed the pills and returned to my "normal" life. The next thing I had to look forward to was a Dave Matthews Band concert.

* * *

In the five days between my release and the concert, my friends had taken turns keeping me busy. My close pal Ryan Schuette came to pick me up from my parents' house—because I wasn't allowed to drive—and took me out. He took me over to the house where we had lived together, and we played whiffle ball in the front yard, shared some laughs, and just hung out. I loved spending time with him and the rest of the guys who lived in that house, but my mind was still slipping into confrontational thoughts.

"I am gonna grab that wheel and jerk this car off the road and kill us both," I said, during the drive.

Ryan laughed at first, thinking I was joking, but when he looked at my face, he could see it was not a laughing matter.

"Wells, you don't want to do that; we are going to the DMB show tomorrow night." We had tickets to see the Dave Matthews Band at the Verizon Wireless Amphitheater.

I was silent and looked out the window. Ryan is like a brother to me, and in my right mind, I would never have threatened his life or mine. I was not well and I wasn't thinking clearly because I was off my meds again. Implosion was just around the corner.

The next night, Ryan and Kate met up with me for concert pregame at our friend Tim Niedringhaus's home, which was near the amphitheater. There was nothing out of the ordinary during the preparty. We all loved the DMB and looked forward to going to their shows every summer. About an hour before the show Ryan, Kate, and I decided to leave Tim's to tailgate in the venue parking lot. We set up our cooler near a red Ford truck and shotgunned cold beers in between taking shots of Jägermeister.

I wasn't just drinking; I was forcing down beer after shot, one right after the other. By the time we walked into the concert, I was well above the legal blood-alcohol limit in Missouri—in any state, for that matter. Mixing all that alcohol so rapidly ignited a fuse of manic rage that was beginning to burn. And I had no medication with me. Bipolar disorder can strike just like asthma; you need immediate medication to get the attack under control.

So, what did I do? I took Kate right to the drink stand to buy two hurricanes. Hurricanes are dangerous: They taste like Kool-Aid and contain 151-proof Everclear, which might as well be rubbing alcohol. I drank mine in a few enormous gulps. Kate didn't like the taste of hers and passed it to me. Two hurricanes in a single night is more than enough to get anyone smashed, let alone two of them in fifteen minutes and after countless cans of beer and Jäger shots. I was mentally mangled beyond repair after those cocktails and the mania was spiking, further fueled by my excitement at seeing one of my favorite bands.

We made our way to the seats for the first few songs. When the band came on, we danced and enjoyed the show. They are the last songs I remember hearing that night. The music stopped and my ears became filled with the sound of an angry, muzzled beehive for the rest of that night. The music was silenced by my mania.

Luckily, there were three empty seats next to me, because I turned to my right and vomited. But I never broke stride; I just turned my head, emptied out all the beer, Jäger, and hurricanes and went right back to dancing. Ryan noticed, but Kate did not. Ryan, again looking out for me, said he was going to the bathroom and asked me to go with him.

While Ryan disappeared into the men's room, I sat outside the bathroom and waited for him. Out of sheer coincidence, I ran into Courtney Hennessey-Hopson, my old roommate from Jupiter who had since married my friend Mike.

When Courtney and I hugged she could tell something was out of whack with me. Ryan came out of the bathroom, and I slapped him across the face for absolutely no reason. It was the only time in my life that I had ever hit anyone in the mania; I had pushed my dad around a few days earlier but never took a swing at him. Ryan didn't know what to do. He was trying to play the babysitter with me, and I attacked him physically and verbally.

"You think you know me? You don't know shit about me!" I barked.

It was like a switch had flipped. All at once, the booze and the lack of medication kicked in. I took a swing at Ryan. Thank goodness he ducked and I missed. In a matter of a few seconds, I had completely turned on one of my best friends.

A security guard appeared suddenly. I kept going after Ryan, but the security guard separated us. He was going to arrest us both when a woman from the concession stand raced over and told the cop that Ryan had done nothing wrong and that I had instigated the entire fight. Courtney witnessed all of it, too, but ran back to her seat not knowing what to do.

The security guard allowed Ryan to leave, but wouldn't let me go anywhere. Two more security guards restrained me with my hands behind my back and told me they were taking me to the amphitheater holding cell. I didn't argue and must have been calm; they didn't put me in handcuffs.

After walking about twenty yards, it hit me that I was going to jail. When the realization set in, I decided to throw an elbow to the head of the security guard on my right. Not a smart move. Before I knew it, the cops had pinned me down and were slapping on the cuffs. With my face pressed against the cement, I vividly recalled a scene from *Good Will Hunting*, in which Matt Damon's character is pinned down, face smashed on the blacktop, after a schoolyard fight. The last thing I remember thinking before blacking out was *Oh fuck, this is gonna hurt*.

The altercation between Ryan and me was so upsetting that Ryan immediately called my parents. He told them that the police would probably be calling them. Ryan's actions are just one example of how great my friends have been over the years in helping me deal with the ups and downs of bipolar disorder. Even after my attack on him, he still cared enough to let my parents know I was in trouble. He knows me at my core and had become fully aware of how much bipolar disorder can twist a person into a mere shadow of themselves. Ryan is a true friend, and I am eternally grateful to him for doing what was best for me even when I tested our friendship; he could have easily given up on me.

* * *

When I woke up from my blackout, I was in a pure white hospital room: White walls, white sink, white examination table, two white chairs, and a doctor dressed in a white coat. I looked down to see that I wore a white gown and no shoes. The doctor examined my eyes and checked my heartbeat.

"Mr. Wellington, you have a concussion and your blood alcohol level was 0.19 when they brought you in here," she told me.

"Where am I?" I was still drunk and had the worst headache I'd ever had. Every heartbeat pounded in my temples with excruciating pain. The concussion hammered away on my brain.

"Barnes Hospital," she told me.

I had absolutely no clue how I got there. I had been in the Maryland Heights Police Department in a holding cell for a few hours before an ambulance transported me to the hospital. My parents spoke with the police and explained that I had bipolar disorder and that they were recently having trouble with me. It was my parents' request that landed me in Barnes Hospital. My new doctor was on staff at Barnes, so it was the logical place to go.

The doctor finished her evaluation, and I was left to wait in the white room by myself. I didn't feel manic or restless; I just felt tired. I fell asleep and then woke myself with my own snoring a handful of times. Eventually, two nurses showed up, put me into a wheelchair, and told me I was being transferred to a different room. They took me to the fifteenth floor.

I would become very familiar with the fifteenth floor.

It was similar to the treatment floor at St. Mary's. Patient rooms along the long hallway, a television viewing area—without couches—with square tables set in perfect order, and a nurses' station that stretched halfway down the hall.

I was placed in a room by myself and went right to sleep. I was completely worn out. When I woke up, I walked out of my room into darkness, except for the light at the nurses' station. I was scared; it was eerily silent.

I approached the desk at the station to find an older woman wearing a tie-dyed shirt underneath her lab coat. She was in her fifties and had a smiling face that put me a little at ease.

"What time is it?" I asked her.

"Two thirty in the morning."

She offered me a caffeine-free soda (caffeine is not allowed in the loony bin). I stood in the dark hall and sipped my soft drink and started to wonder what the hell I had gotten myself into. I went back to my room, lay on the bed, and became angry. I was sick of being trapped in a hospital—first St. Mary's and now Barnes. I wasn't sure how long I would be there. This would be another involuntary commitment. Did that mean three more days?

Any day on the fifteenth floor at Barnes is agonizing. You are alone with only your thoughts. It was difficult to ask myself *Why me?* On a typical day in June, I would be spending seven or eight hours a day outside in the sun, working on my golf game or teaching lessons. Now, I was stuck indoors, freezing and yearning to be outside with the blue skies and warm sun. If hell existed, I was convinced it would have to be bitterly cold.

My medication hadn't completely stabilized my mania within the first twenty-four hours, so my first day on the floor, I paced up and down the forty-yard-long hall. My anger was reaching a boiling point; I felt like a caged animal.

I was surly and nasty toward the staff. I was asked by several doctors on the floor to participate in therapy groups. My response to each of them was as ugly and demeaning as words could be.

"I don't need to listen to anything you guys have to say! I will be out of here soon enough, and then I never have to deal with you fuckers ever again!" I hissed at one of the nurses as I paced up and down the hall.

The lithium and a separate sedative administered every night before bed finally took effect. By the fourth day, I began to return to my right mind, even though I was still frustrated to be stuck in a cage like a rabbit.

Eventually, I began to level out and to become friendly with some of the nurses. By the fifth day, I was to be discharged after meeting with my new doctor—Dr. Robert Cloninger, who Dan Finney had recommended.

* * *

This stay at Barnes would turn out to be the most important hospital stay that I have ever had because it was the beginning of years of therapy with Dr. Cloninger. Dr. Robert Cloninger is world renowned. He has published books, given seminars, and traveled the world in search of finding ways to help his patients deal with mental illness. He is an expert in the science of well-being.

My first meeting with him was in a room that was no bigger than a hotel bathroom. We sat only a few feet apart from one another on cushioned chairs that looked like they belonged at my grandmother's dining room table. Dr. Cloninger is a tall, slender man, about six foot two, with white hair and a white beard and mustache. He speaks slowly and laughs often. The fact that he had worked with Dan Finney was a big deal to me; that connection eased my anxiety about trusting him.

My first order of business was to request that we try a different medication. I wanted to get off lithium. This was really a bad idea. The lithium had been extremely successful from mid-2001 through the first few months of 2004. The problem was me not taking it.

Dr. Cloninger suggested Depakote, a very well-known bipolar medication. I eagerly agreed to try it. He wanted to meet with my parents and me the day after my release. I just wanted to get the hell out of the cage, so I agreed.

My dad picked me up from Barnes the following morning, and we spent the first five minutes of the car ride in silence. I resented my parents because I felt that they had begun the chain reaction of the last two hospital visits.

He broke the silence.

"Michael, you are a great kid, and we hate to see you in the hospital. But you are the only person who can keep you out of there; all you need to do is take your medicine."

At that moment, I could hear the sincerity and pain in his voice. But my lame "I know" response was cold.

When we arrived at their house, my mom and I exchanged dirty looks as I came into the kitchen. She grew up in a strong-willed Irish–German family on the South Side of Chicago and has a strong personality—she doesn't take any shit. Her father and grandfather were both high-ranking officials of the Beer and Soft Drink Workers Union of Chicago, and she was one of six children. They were hard-nosed, no-nonsense kind of people, and that rubbed off on my mom.

I knew that I wouldn't be able to live at my parents' house for very long because of the tension that was already bubbling between us.

I was again not allowed to drive a car for the first seven days after my release from the hospital. As usual, my friends took turns picking me up and getting me back into life. Kate was awesome about the whole experience. My bipolar disorder was now out in the open, and we talked candidly about managing it properly.

The Depakote side effects added an unexpected layer of difficulty. The first time Kate picked me up after I started the Depakote was quite a scene. On our way to visit my former roommates after hanging out at her house for a couple of hours, I opened the passenger door while stopped at a stop sign and vomited all over the street. The nausea came out of nowhere. All bipolar medications are strong, and it is normally recommended that they be taken with food or with a glass of milk to buffer the stomach, but I had taken my Depakote without any food. I threw up again when we got to the boys' house.

I think the vomiting made my struggle with bipolar disorder more immediate and physical to Kate, which led to us slowly losing touch. I obviously wasn't stable, and she knew I needed to be alone to work on myself. I have tremendous respect for her and will always be grateful for her helping me through that dark period, but our relationship was doomed before it really had a chance to begin.

The next afternoon, I went to pick up some fast food in the hopes of padding my stomach before taking the Depakote. Twenty minutes after taking the medication, I pulled my car over and threw up again. So it wasn't the lack of food.

I immediately called Dr. Cloninger's office to set up an appointment. He was able to get me in the next day. I told him what was happening, and he got out his medication journal and looked up the known effects of Depakote; ten percent of the people who take Depakote experience violent vomiting. I went back to lithium.

* * *

The situation at my parents' house was not good. We couldn't have a conversation without it escalating into a yelling match. I needed to find another place to live or my mom and I were going to drive each other crazy. At the end of June, my good friend Bryan Pilkington, who everyone calls "Pilk," offered to rent me a room at his new apartment in the Maplewood neighborhood in the heart of St. Louis. I moved in immediately, putting some much-needed space between my mom and me.

I stabilized again and threw all my energy into working on my golf game. I began to appreciate the game even more because it had been taken from me while I was in the hospital. I was angry about the lost time and motivated to make up for it.

By August, my golf game was starting to take off. I had been on lithium again for six weeks, and my mind was back to a stable state. So, I started preparing for Q-School.

I began playing in a Friday afternoon money game at The Country Club at The Legends, in Eureka, Missouri. It was a big game, usually around twenty to thirty guys, and you could leave the course with a few hundred dollars if you played well. The Legends is a tough Robert Trent Jones, Jr., layout that is tight off the tee and has many water hazards that collect errant shots.

In mid-August, I finally played a round that made Q-School seem like a good move again. I played the front nine in 31, five under par. I made birdies at ten and eleven, par on twelve, and birdies on thirteen and fourteen. One of my playing partners, Chris Collins, flat out asked me, "Mike, how many under are you?" as the rest were adding up my shots out loud. Right there, I knew my momentum was at risk.

"Not sure," I said. "Who is keeping the card?" I was trying my best to play one shot at a time and not get distracted by the score.

"I have you at nine under." Mike Woods was keeping all our scores on the little scoring pad on the steering wheel of his golf cart.

Up to that point I had been in the moment; now I was focusing on the shots to come. Well, if I make birdie on this hole I can shoot . . . If I make three more birdies, I can shoot . . . If I make all pars from here to the club-house, I'll shoot 63 . . .

As with any activity that requires concentration, golfers can destroy their game by getting hung up on a bad shot or score. If a golfer is to get the most out of their mental game, they must stay in the present, which is much easier said than done.

I made two bogeys on the way in and shot 65, still seven under par.

When I pulled out of the parking lot at The Legends, I was on cloud nine. You have to build on all great rounds, especially when you only play ten or fifteen tournament rounds in a year. I couldn't stop thinking about reaching nine under through fourteen holes, a major accomplishment for me. It was a glimpse of the potential that I always believed I had but had never reached before that day. It was a tour player's round.

Two weeks later, I did it again—this time in Aspen. I was in the mountains with a large group from St. Louis for a wedding. On the morning of the rehearsal dinner, I set up a money game at the Aspen Golf Club with Pilk, my old good luck charm Gary Pohrer, and our friend Kevin McLaughlin after a late night of drinking and partying.

The four of us got to the course five minutes before tee time—no time to warm up or hit any practice putts. I made birdie on the first hole, par on number two, birdie at number three, and par again on the fourth hole. On number five, I cold shanked my second shot from underneath a tree but got it up and down from seventy-five yards to save par. I made par again on six, birdied seven and eight, and saved par at nine to turn in four under—31—for the round. The holes seemed to be the size of basketball hoops; I only needed ten putts on the first nine holes. I started the back nine with birdies at ten, eleven, and twelve.

I forced myself not to think about my score, even though I knew I was going really low. This time around, no one mentioned anything about my playing. I made par on thirteen, fourteen, fifteen, and sixteen.

On the seventeenth tee, we had a long wait for the group in front of us—time enough to realize I had a career round going. My nerves got to me, and I hooked my tee shot thirty yards left of the green, behind two huge pine trees.

When I turned my head I saw Hoffy on the fourth green, adjacent to the seventeenth tee box. I jogged over and waited for his group to finish putting.

"Hoffy! What's up, my man?"

"Mikey? Is that you, kid? You put on a few pounds!"

He gave me a warm hug, and we caught up for a minute. I had so much respect for him, even more so after he had called me out at Maroon Creek. It would be the last time I'd ever see Hoffy. He died a year later in his sleep.

We parted ways, and I returned to the trouble I had gotten myself into on the seventeenth hole. I couldn't even see the green because I was blocked by the two ten-foot-tall pine trees. If I tried to go right at the hole, the pine on the left would block my ball. I'd have to hit an enormous flop shot through the opening between the tops of the two trees in the hope of getting my ball on the front of the green, about thirty feet from the hole.

I opened up my trusty sixty-degree wedge and made the biggest swing I could. My ball rose straight up, just missing a branch of the pine on the left, then disappeared through the opening and landed on the front edge of the green. I couldn't have done any better. Now I had to make a thirty-five-foot putt to save my par and stay at seven under for the day.

I took my time reading my putt as Gary was lining up for his third birdie on the back nine. He missed it and tapped in for par. I kept my head still and made a pure roll that broke from left to right, then veered back to the left in the second half of the line. It had perfect speed and dove into the middle of the hole for a miraculous par to tie Gary on the hole.

"You motherfucker!" he exclaimed. "Are you gonna miss one today?"

I wore an ear-to-ear grin as we walked to the eighteenth tee. The last hole at the Aspen Golf Club is a medium-size par four that requires a good drive and a nine iron into the green. I caught my approach shot a little fat and wound up twenty-five feet short of the hole. Gary hit a great second shot and had only twelve feet left for his birdie. When I got to the green, I didn't take much time to read the putt—I just felt I was going to make it. Sure enough, I rolled it in.

Gary erupted. "You are a real asshole!" he said with a smile.

I shot 63, tied the course record and won every bet that was on the table. But I was most proud that I had stayed in the moment to finish off the round, a lesson I kept with me from the weak finish at The Legends. Seeing Hoffy for the last time also made the round memorable. It seems fitting that our last encounter was on the golf course during one of the best rounds I have ever played.

* * *

I made the decision to take another stab at Martin Downs in Palm City, Florida, where I had endured my Q-School disaster a year earlier. I knew the course well and would have Mullin caddie for me again.

I felt good. I had a caddie that I trusted and who knew my game, I was very familiar with the golf course, and I had been playing the best golf of my life for the past two months. I was taking my lithium every morning, and the consistency of the medication in my system was contributing to my consistency on the golf course.

I could do it.

The four rounds at this first stage of Q-School were squeezed into three days because late October is hurricane season in south Florida, and one was forecast to sweep through Palm City on the fourth day.

I was full of nerves at the beginning of my first round. I hadn't played a competitive round since the disaster at the US Open qualifier. It took me about four holes to settle and get into the round. I made a sloppy double bogey on number three, a 495-yard par four that seems like it always plays into the wind. The wind howls at Martin Downs, and you have to pick the right club, angle your ball low, and control its trajectory while guessing how the wind will affect your shot. I ended up shooting 74 for the day

The second day was a race against darkness—thankfully, outside rather than in my mind—to fit in twenty-seven holes. I finally got going on the sixth hole after starting the round with five pars. The sixth hole at Martin Downs is a 380-yard par four that was playing into a thirty-mile-per-hour wind. I played my driver to the right side of the fairway, leaving 128 yards to the hole looking right into the gale force. Mullin and I decided I should play a punch eight-iron shot. Normally, with no wind, an eight iron would yield a 155- to 160-yard shot, but in these strong breezes, you had to be creative. The knock-down eight iron proved to be the perfect club. The shot never left the flagstick and finished two inches from the hole for a tap-in birdie. Building on that momentum, I made par on number seven, birdied the par-five eighth, and chipped in for birdie at nine to shoot 33 on the front. The back nine of the second round was rock solid, even though we played the last four holes in a light rain with heavier storms brewing. Eight pars and a birdie added up to 35—a 68 for the second round. Now we were in the mix.

We began our third round on the tenth tee, trying to squeeze the extra nine holes into the second day. We were paired with Jim Herman, whose playing inspired me. I made birdie on number ten with a twenty-foot putt and navigated the blustery wind on the eleventh hole with a solid par.

The twelfth hole is a 445-yard par four with out-of-bounds down the entire right side. I subconsciously guided my tee shot into the fairway bunker; it was a better option than risking the out-of-bounds down the right side. Sometimes, a competitive golfer's mind instinctively forces a player away from trouble to avoid penalty strokes. If only the bipolar mind could do the same!

As Mullin and I got to my ball in the sand, the inclement weather horn blew—lightning. I marked my ball's position in the bunker with two tees, and we went back to the clubhouse to take shelter. The wait was agonizing. I had been playing so well that I wanted to keep going. The delay lasted about an hour before we could finally head back to the number-twelve fairway bunker.

We had had perfect, calm conditions in the wake of the storm. I had 155 yards to the hole, so I grabbed an eight iron and picked the shot clean off the sand to within ten feet of the hole. I made the putt for another birdie. Now we were really in the hunt. I made a scrambling par on number thirteen and a testy little seven-foot putt for par on number fourteen. I made a routine par on the fifteenth. At sixteen, I drove my ball perfectly into the middle of the fairway and left myself a short wedge shot for the approach, but I missed the green to the left and chipped to a nervous distance of six feet. It was almost dark, and sixteen would most likely be our final hole of the day. I rolled in the six-footer, ending the day with my momentum high as we faced twenty-nine holes the next day. I felt really good about the comeback I had made after the shaky first round.

We had to get to the course extra early for the 7:15 restart on the final day. We began on the seventeenth tee, a reachable par five. I missed a five-foot putt for birdie and let it get to me, consequently making bogey on eighteen. But, I was still under par for my third round. My back nine was uneventful: seven pars, a birdie, and a bogey to finish with a 70.

We were in a golf marathon of thirty-six holes in twenty-five hours, with eighteen left to play. It was the first time I had a legitimate chance to advance through the first stage of Q-School.

Mullin and I went to the locker room to relax a bit before the final round. We figured we had about an hour and a half before we would go back out for the fourth round. Mullin went out to check the scoreboard while I took a brief nap. Within twenty minutes of closing my eyes, Mullin burst back into the locker room.

"Michael! Michael! We are on the tee in twelve minutes!"

"What? I thought we had over an hour?"

"No, let's go!"

We made our way to the first tee in a big hurry, with no time for practice balls. I was nervous, my heart was pounding, and I was moving too fast as I faced the first hole, a 430-yard par four with a parking lot and out-of-bounds to the right of the fairway and tall palm trees guarding the left side of the hole. I blocked my ball well right of the fairway, toward the out-of-bounds stakes near the parking lot. The ball landed six inches out of bounds. I had to take a two-stroke penalty and hit another tee shot. I couldn't afford to make any more mistakes and had to focus.

I found the fairway with my second tee shot but missed the green with my next. I played a so-so bump-and-run shot to within eight feet of the hole. It was a huge putt. I could recover from a double bogey, but a triple bogey would probably put me out of the running. To this day, I have never been more nervous standing over a putt. I told myself to keep my head still until I heard Mullin and the other people in our group react to the putt. I wasn't going to watch it roll. I went through my routine and put what I felt was a good stroke on the putt and then just listened . . .

"Atta, boy!" I heard Mullin and then looked up, but my ball had disappeared.

I pulled off four straight pars after the opening-hole debacle. On number six, I finally made a birdie, sinking a twenty-foot right-to-left snake that dove into the hole as if it was hunting for mouse. That putt put a little pep in my step. I made par on seven and eight but made a costly bogey on number nine when I missed a five-foot putt. I would have to play a good back nine in order to sneak through to the second stage.

On number ten I knocked my approach shot from 124 yards to five feet with a pitching wedge and drained the putt for a bounce-back birdie. The treacherous par-three eleventh hole loomed in front of me, and the wind was howling in my face. I played a four iron through the breeze to the back of the green. If my four iron came up short, I'd wind up in the water. I two-putted for a rock-solid par and got the hell out of there. Routine pars followed on twelve, thirteen, and fourteen. I missed the green on fifteen and failed to save par. That bogey was a dagger.

On sixteen, I made par and narrowly missed a twenty-five-foot birdie putt. I needed a birdie and fast. My tee shot on the par-five seventeenth hole found a fairway bunker, and I was forced to lay up to 104 yards. I played my sand wedge for the third shot to ten feet. I studied the birdie try from every angle. It was a little bit downhill, which was good because it would be hard to leave the putt short of the hole. It would move left to right. It wasn't a very difficult putt except for the circumstances. I stuck to my routine—kept my head down after the putt—but this time I looked up to watch the last two feet of the putt roll out.

I shouldn't have looked. My ball was rolling with good speed, took the break that I had anticipated, looked into the right side of the hole, grabbed the right edge of the cup, went down for a split second, then came back up like a baby spitting out a pacifier. Mullin was the first to react.

"You cocksucker!" He blurted out at the ball while shaking the flagstick over his head.

I didn't react verbally, but I was pissed. I hit a great putt that didn't fall. Now I absolutely had to make birdie on the last hole.

There are no scoreboards at Q-School, so you never know where you stand in relation to the rest of the field. But I could feel that I needed a birdie. The eighteenth hole at Martin Downs is a dangerous hole. It's a 420-yard par four, but you can't hit a driver because the fairway runs out at around 250 yards where a large lake swallows tee shots that are too aggressive. I played a three wood from the tee and left myself 185 yards to the hole from the left side of the fairway. The hole was cut in the back-middle portion of the green, so the water really wasn't in play. I hit a six-iron shot that was hole-high about fifteen feet left of the hole on the fringe—an excellent shot under the circumstances.

I was faced with another must-make shot. Mullin and I read the putt and decided it would move right to left, so I would start it a ball's width outside the hole to hook it into the cup. I kept my head still as I stroked the putt. My shoulders rocked back and through with the stroke, and it felt like a solid strike in the middle of the putter face. The putt never broke left. It missed just to the right of the cup and rolled a foot past. I tapped in for par, but I could feel that it wouldn't be good enough to qualify. We made our way to the scoreboard to find out.

I had shot rounds of 74–68–70–74 and missed advancing by two strokes. It was a twenty-one-stroke improvement from my prior trip to Q-School the year before at the same golf course, but it still wasn't good enough.

The top twenty scores and ties would advance to the second stage. I had tied for twenty-second place. When we confirmed that I was outside the placing, I felt like I had the wind knocked out of me. There were so many shots that I had left out on the golf course that it made me sick. I immediately recalled having to rush to the first tee of the final round, hitting that tee shot out of bounds, costing me two shots.

When a golfer reflects on a round of eighteen holes, they can always recall at least one instance where they let a shot or multiple shots slip away. When fighting for your life at Q-School, those mistakes become magnified in your mind.

It took me a few hours to cool off, and I found a few positives about what I had done during the week. I had shown improvement, even though I hadn't played any real tournaments that entire summer and fall. I hadn't made any horrible mistakes coming down the stretch and had maintained a chance until the last few holes when the pressure became the most intense.

I definitely wanted another chance, and as I made the two-day, twenty-hour drive back to St. Louis, I looked forward to next year's Q-School.

For now, I was out of money and needed to find a job.

THE FOURTEEN CLUBS

I slipped into mania in 2004 because I hadn't stuck to my routine. I went off my meds, didn't sleep, and drank heavily. Only when I was forced to reincorporate medication into my routine did I start to emerge from the mania. I also discovered therapy during my hospital stay, and it has proven indispensable in keeping me healthy.

5

BASEBALL AND BARNES—
JEWISH HOSPITAL

*I put my heart and soul into my work and
have lost my mind in the process.
—Vincent Van Gogh*

MY MOM ALWAYS thought I should give up my golf career and go
into broadcasting. I have a voice and a laugh that carry well, and I tend to
get loud when I get excited. In fact, one of the favorite nicknames I have
been given over the years is "Yellington."

Sports broadcasting maintains a strong hold on the St. Louis commu-
nity—so it's had a strong hold on me. Harry Caray worked in St. Louis
before going to the Chicago Cubs; Dan Kelly, the greatest broadcaster in
the history of the city, called Blues hockey games with an unmatched zest.
I have tuned in to Cardinals games on KMOX since I was three years old,
listening to the legendary duo of Jack Buck and Mike Shannon call the
plays. Bob Costas grew to become a favorite of mine at a young age when I
saw him on all the major networks. Jack Buck's son Joe came on to the St.
Louis broadcasting scene in the early1990s. His talent turned him into a
titan in both the local and national broadcasting business.

When I was in college, I interned at my friend Tim Dorsey's new radio
station, The Big 550, KTRS (the TRS stands for "Tim's radio station").
I interned for Kevin Slaten, "The King of St. Louis Sports Talk Radio."
I learned a lot from him during my apprenticeship, and being around a
natural talent like him was a great experience.

Jim Nantz is another broadcasting great I admired. As a high school kid,
I would come home drunk after a night out and retreat to the basement to
watch a VHS recording of the 1986 Masters, with Jim Nantz announcing.
I must have watched that tape hundreds of times and loved Nantz's gem

while calling the sixteenth hole after Nicklaus made birdie: "There is no doubt about it, the Bear . . . has come out of hibernation."

So, after not being able to continue into the next stage at Q-School, I looked into getting into the broadcasting business. I knew I would go back to golf at some point, but I needed to do something to appease my mom and to occupy my time until my next chance, so I enrolled at the Broadcast Center of St. Louis in November 2005.

The Broadcast Center offers a nine-month program that is well known for producing quality broadcasters. Once you've completed the program, the center guarantees your placement in a broadcasting job somewhere in the United States. By mid-November, I was knee deep in learning tricks of the trade, such as inflection, tone, proper breathing, and technical work; in December, I got a job offer that I couldn't refuse.

One of my dearest friends, Tony Vitello, was a baseball coach at the University of Missouri. Tony knew I was going to the Broadcast Center and asked me if I would be available to become the color commentator for the 2006 Missouri Tiger Baseball program. This was a chance to fulfill a childhood dream of calling baseball. I would have to quit the Broadcast Center, because the job with Missouri would require travel all over the Big 12 Conference, but not until February when the baseball season began. This wasn't just a job; it was a dream job.

I would be calling all the games in the press box alongside long-time Mizzou baseball play-by-play legend Tex Little. Calling baseball games came rather naturally to me; I was good at telling the story of what I saw. There is also a lot of dead time in baseball, so we would fill it with conversation. Tex had been calling Mizzou games for more than fourteen years at that point, so I made sure to ask him about past Tiger greats when we had a lull in the action.

I began traveling with the team at the end of February. The broadcasting job gave me such a high that I quit taking my medicine at the end of February. My ego was on the loose again.

* * *

After securing the broadcasting job with Mizzou, I got a second job at the beginning of March 2006 at Stonewolf Golf Club, in Fairview Heights,

Illinois. My job with the baseball team was a dream, but it didn't pay very well, and the baseball season and the broadcasting job would end in June.

I met with Walter Wolfner, the owner of Stonewolf at the time and convinced him to hire me as an independent contractor; I would act as the director of golf instruction at the club and would keep all my lesson revenue in exchange for helping out during the large corporate outings that Stonewolf hosted. That meant I could set my own schedule and be at the club on my own time. I could play the course and practice when I wanted, as well. It was a sweet deal for me, but the job also had another big perk. By working there, I would be able to play in all the Gateway PGA Section tournaments around Southern Illinois and St. Louis, giving me an opportunity to keep my golf game sharp.

The Gateway PGA Section events were typically held on Mondays. Players are made up of the PGA club and teaching professionals who work at the country clubs and public golf facilities in Southern Illinois and the St. Louis metropolitan area. Bob Gaus is a legend of the Gateway Section. In his thirty years of playing, he has qualified for two US Opens and four PGA Championships and has advanced to the final stage of Q-School. J. C. Anderson also competed in these events; he played the PGA Tour for a number of years before getting back into teaching. He is a pro's pro, and I loved being paired with him, which made me play at a higher level than my regular game.

There were many more serious competitors within the Section. My swing teacher, Rob Sedorcek, from the Country Club at St. Alban's; Garth Bayer, the head pro at Old Warson Country Club; Steve Lotz, the head pro at Tower Tee Golf Center; Mike Tucker, the head professional at Bellerive Country Club; Mark Faulkner, Lake of Egypt owner; Brian Norman, Crab Orchard assistant pro; Nash Haxel, Glen Echo head pro; Ryan Roy, Norwood Hills head pro; Brett Moomey, head pro at Old Hickory; and my good friend and the director of instruction at Whitmoor Country Club, Bobby Pavelonis. I knew that playing with this caliber of player every week would only help me improve.

Pavelonis was familiar with my bipolar condition and had always been very supportive of me because bipolar disorder runs in his family, too. He has stayed on me over the years about the importance of taking my medicine.

"You been taking your medicine, Michael?" He would ask me often.

"Yeah, Bobby. Have you been taking yours?" I would answer with a smile.

But before I could compete in the Gateway Section events against all these great players, I would have to pass the PAT, otherwise known as the Play Ability Test in the beginning of April. I had a good month to get organized with both jobs and figure out a routine.

* * *

Now I had two jobs: The baseball gig was an hour-and-a-half drive west of St. Louis, in Columbia, and the teaching job was thirty-five minutes east of the city. Bouncing back and forth among Columbia, St. Louis, and Fairview Heights, I was constantly on the move and loved every second of it.

The first month with the baseball team was a great success. The team crushed its opponents every week. We traveled to Gainesville, Florida, where we beat the then-number-one-ranked Florida Gators on their home turf. The Missouri lineup was loaded with future major-league talent. Our best pitcher, Max Scherzer, would eventually be a first-round draft pick for the Arizona Diamondbacks and would go on to win the Cy Young award in 2013 with the Detroit Tigers. The Diamondbacks also drafted our most talented outfielder, Evan Frey, and our best infielder, Brock Bond, went on to play in the San Francisco Giants organization.

The coaching staff was a great mix of talent and experience as well. Third-base coach Evan Pratt had major-league experience with the Detroit Tigers. Outfield coach Luke Cassius had a great ability to keep players loose. Graduate assistant coach Kevin Cullen had a very studied approach to the game and went on to become a talent scout for the Cleveland Indians. We had the best student manager in the business, Paul Kruger, who went to the Texas Rangers' front office. Each of those great minds meshed well with the smooth and cerebral approach of head coach Tim Jamieson to create a special chemistry for the team, bolstered by Vitello's never-ending fire and hunger to win. The 2006 Tigers had all the tools to reach the College World Series in Omaha, Nebraska, in June.

I was allowed to bring my golf clubs on all the road trips. I could practice during the day because most of our games were at night. Did I mention that this was a great job?

My weekly schedule was packed. We played three-game series with each opponent. When we traveled to away games—a Friday night game, a Saturday afternoon game, and a Sunday game around 11:00 a.m.—I would have to be in Columbia on Thursday afternoon. We'd return to Columbia on Sunday evening, and I would usually get back to St. Louis late Sunday night. For home games, I would have to be in Columbia about two hours before the Friday afternoon game. Saturday home games were usually in the afternoon, and Sunday's were always around noon. If we won on Sunday, there was always a celebration at Tony's house that night, and I would stay in his spare bedroom. If we lost, I would head back to St. Louis immediately after the game was over. I couldn't handle Tony after a loss. Tony hated to lose more than anyone; it put him in a horrible mood. He had even been that way when we played high school basketball, and he was the last man on the bench.

My baseball schedule left me Monday through Thursday—and sometimes Friday morning—to teach golf lessons at Stonewolf.

No bipolar issues rose to the surface at the end of February or in March, but as April blossomed, so did my hypomania, the period just before mania strikes. It was just a matter of time before I crossed over.

* * *

Life was moving fast: I was traveling all over the country with the team, working long hours at Stonewolf teaching lessons, and working hard on my own golf game in any spare daylight hours. My nightlife was on the rise too. Winning Sunday nights in Columbia were booze festivals. Wednesday and Thursday nights in St. Louis were reserved for carousing all over town, abusing alcohol, and chasing random women. I was living in the fast lane and feeling invincible.

Then I met Hope.

I met her on a Wednesday night when I was out with the boys. We were having drinks at our favorite sushi spot in downtown Clayton. As I was walking to the bathroom I noticed a group of girls on a purple velvet couch. Hope was sitting on the arm of the couch, smiling and laughing. She didn't see me when I walked past, but on my return trip, we locked eyes and kept them locked until I reached her. I smiled and began my bullshit.

"I'm Michael. What's your name?" She was the most gorgeous woman I had ever seen. She had on tight blue jeans, a white V-neck T-shirt that showed a little bit of cleavage, black heels, and some cool bracelets and rings. It was an outfit that was stylish and sexy but low maintenance and relaxed. She had short, bleach-blonde hair, big brown eyes, and curves like Scarlett Johansson. She had a fun and giddy energy and seemed genuinely happy.

"I'm Hope. I like your hat!" She grabbed my royal blue Brooklyn Dodgers hat right off my head and put it on. She couldn't have known it, but I have a thing for a girl in a baseball cap. We had immediate chemistry. The conversation flowed so easily—there was none of the typical awkward bar banter. She was real. She wasn't pretentious. She had an electrifying smile, and it was literally difficult to keep my hands off her. I felt like I had known her forever.

Before I knew it, the lights came on signaling closing time. We talked our respective groups of friends into heading to a late-night bar to continue the evening. When the boys and I arrived, the girls were parked outside the bar. I walked up to the driver's side window of the white SUV, with Hope in the driver's seat. She rolled down her window.

"We have to leave. One of my girlfriends has to work early, and it's already 1:45."

"Can I have your number? We should definitely hang out again."

She gave me her number and I put it in my cell phone. Then I kissed her. I couldn't help myself. We kissed long enough for her girlfriends in the backseat to "Ewwwww!" at us in unison.

Hope smiled and drove away without a word. Damn, she was sexy!

I was already smitten. I had to leave the next day for Columbia for the weekend baseball games, so I couldn't see her until the following week, but I courted her via text message in between innings.

Me: *What's up with the coolest girl in school today?*
Hope: *When are you back in St. Louis?*
Me: *As soon as possible. Are we going to dinner?*
Hope: *Yep! :)*

God bless technology! When I got back to St. Louis on the following Sunday night, Hope told me over dinner that she was a hairstylist. On the spot I made an appointment for Tuesday. That night I knew that I was done chasing the ladies. I had to make her my girlfriend.

I was on a high. I had a play-by-play broadcasting job with an NCAA Division I college baseball team, I was the director of golf instruction at a Jack Nicklaus Signature Design golf facility, and I was in hot pursuit of a gorgeous and cool girl. No mania, no hospitals, no lithium. Life was awesome!

* * *

My Missouri Tigers were having a great season, and I loved my time in the broadcast booth. I was skipping my lithium and hiding it well—I couldn't see any problems looming. Looking back, I can see that my bipolar issues were getting ready to take hold again.

As March turned into April, things were heating up with Hope. We spent almost every night together whenever I was in St. Louis—going to movies, late suppers, or concerts. We regularly stayed out until three o'clock in the morning, searching for the best jukeboxes in St. Louis. We couldn't get enough of each other.

The only time I slept was when I passed out on the couch in Pilk's basement. It was typically a late afternoon crash, timed so I didn't miss a night out. I stayed out late on weeknights in St. Louis with Hope or drinking and occasionally going to strip clubs in Southwestern Illinois with the boys. I spent most Friday and Saturday nights out late on the road. The schedule was terrible for my sleep habits. The constant travel, excessive drinking at least four nights a week, and minimal hours of sleep were creating a brand new mania that would become so large it could have had its own zip code. I lived like this for a solid month, functioning on hypomanic energy that approached full-blown mania by the hour.

After a short time together, Hope began to ask if our relationship was going anywhere. I hadn't yet told her about my disorder: I was afraid of losing her because of what she might have heard about the disease. There are so many people who are very quick to judge what a bipolar person's life is like based on little knowledge, experience, or research.

We had our first intense conversation on April 7, 2006, after game one of the Tigers three-game series at home against the Nebraska Cornhuskers.

When I left St. Louis for Columbia, I could tell that things with Hope were headed in the wrong direction.

"Mike, I don't think I want to continue this anymore." She sounded anxious.

I was on my cell phone, pacing around under the lights in the right-field foul territory.

"Why?" I pleaded with her. "I know I want to be with you. I want to introduce you to my parents, and I want you to meet my brother and sister. I only want to be with you. I am not interested in anyone else."

"I'm not sure, Mike. I don't know if this can go any further."

That was the last thing I wanted to hear.

"Can we talk in person when I get back to town on Sunday night?"

"Yeah, that's fine, but I'm pretty sure this is the right thing."

"I understand. I will call you when I am on my way back to St. Louis on Sunday."

When I got off the phone, I was frantic. I had finally found a girl that I wanted to be with, and she was having second thoughts. I immediately called Vitello and told him that I had to go back to St. Louis. I said I would be back in the morning in time for game two. I wouldn't get there until after midnight, but I had to see Hope. This impulsive dash to St. Louis should have been a warning sign that my mania was brimming, but when the bipolar mind becomes fixated on something, there is no stopping it.

I drove directly to her apartment and knocked on the door, but no one was home. I had to let her know that I was there, so I went back to my car and found a yellow legal pad; I would leave her a note. I went back into the apartment building and lay down on the floor in the hallway outside of her apartment and wrote the letter—more odd behavior.

While I was in the middle of penning the note, Hope's roommate and her boyfriend found me on the floor as they returned from a night out. I acknowledged them and proceeded to finish my love letter. The boyfriend made some wisecrack, but I ignored him.

"Where's your girlfriend?" He said in the voice of a seventh grader.

Beat it, nerd.

When I finally completed the note, I knocked on the door and gave it to Hope's roommate. I was a little paranoid that she wouldn't give it to her, but I didn't see another option. I went back to my apartment and crashed. It was the best night of sleep I had gotten in two months.

Hope thanked me the following morning for the letter. She said it helped her realize how serious I was about the relationship. She liked that I was so aggressive in the hopes of saving our budding connection with one another, so she stayed with me. But she was still in the dark about my disorder.

I drove back to Columbia, rejuvenated for the rest of the weekend series and excited that I had averted disaster with Hope. Life was good again.

We lost the last two games of the series against Nebraska, and I had to get back to St. Louis right after the series finale because I had to prepare for my Play Ability Test for the Gateway PGA Section. I needed to practice. By passing the PAT—thirty-six holes in one day—I could compete in the Section immediately.

* * *

When I got back to St. Louis, Hope and I spent every free moment we had with each other. We went out the night before the PAT—just like any other night we stayed out until four o'clock in the morning. Since I needed to be on the first tee at Paradise Valley Golf Course at 7:20, I didn't sleep for a minute. After leaving Hope, I lay awake in my bed for a few hours with my CD player blaring Counting Crows. By six o'clock, I was out the door and on my way to Paradise Valley.

Somehow, I managed to shoot 74–71 over the thirty-six-hole test, which qualified me to play in the Section by eleven shots. When I left the golf course, I almost fell asleep at the wheel as I drove home, but I made it. I was excited. Now I could compete against great players every week, and the tournaments fit my schedule perfectly, never interfering with my broadcasting job.

I shot 73 and finished in a tie for second place under nasty cold and windy conditions in my first Section event. The finish was good for a paycheck of $645 and I needed every penny. That event was held at Forest Hills, the scene of my US Open qualifier debacle a year earlier, and finishing well felt like a bit of redemption. But things were about to get weird.

* * *

In mid-April the Tigers played a three-game set against the Oklahoma Sooners in Norman, Oklahoma. We took the lead in the first game of the series, but the Sooners made a bold comeback and rallied to beat us in the late innings. We squandered a two-run lead in the bottom of the ninth inning in the second game. Losing game two was a knife in the back to our team. But we still had one opportunity to save face and leave Norman with a win. The third game was an even bigger blow to the team's confidence. We made it to the ninth inning with a three-run lead, but the Sooners rattled off four runs to beat us again. The bus ride back to Columbia was silent.

We squandered a great opportunity to sweep the Sooners on their own turf. I took it upon myself to do something to change our mojo. I started doing voodoo.

I thought that voodoo might change our fortunes as a team and point us in a different direction. I didn't tell anyone that I was going to try it. It was a silent move to change our karma for the greater good of the team.

Inspired by Pedro Cerrano's voodoo god Jobu in my favorite baseball movie *Major League*, I went to the Wal-Mart near the apartment I shared with Pilk and bought a Ken doll.

With this Ken doll, I can change the universe and the vibe for our team.

I wrapped green and white St. Patrick's Day beads (for good luck) around the doll's neck like a noose and hung it from a hanger in my closet, behind all my golf shirts. The voodoo doll would be symbolic of every upcoming opponent we would face on the baseball diamond.

The voodoo worked right away. We buried St. Louis University in the next game. We won our second game in a row at home in the first game against Oklahoma State. We lost game two of the series but won the third. We won three out of four and got our boat moving downstream. My manic experimentation with voodoo seemed to be working.

Then we traveled to Kansas City and pummeled Southeast Missouri State 14–3 behind a great performance on the mound by Scherzer. Then made our way home to Taylor Stadium, where we won two out of three against Baylor, grabbed a Tuesday night victory from Missouri State, and then swept Mississippi Valley State.

Our record was 9 and 2 since I put a hex on the opposition, but the voo-doo wasn't helping my golf very much. Before traveling with the Tigers to Lubbock to face Texas Tech, I had another crack at qualifying for the US Open, but I missed advancing to the sectional by five shots.

I turned my focus 100 percent back to the baseball team. We were get-ting into the home stretch of conference play and needed to make a push for the postseason. I still practiced and worked on my golf game, but I wanted to do everything I could to help this team to punch a ticket to Omaha and earn a berth in the College World Series.

The Texas Tech series proved to be a step backward. The Red Raiders swept us, and we had another ninth-inning collapse from a lead in the second game.

When I got back to St. Louis, I went straight to my closet and turned the voodoo doll upside down, hung it up by its ankles. It was time for another fresh start. It worked: We demolished the University of Illinois 14–2 in a Tuesday night game.

* * *

Our final Big 12 Conference series was at home against the University of Texas Longhorns, a perennial national powerhouse. It was the final series for the seniors on the team. I had special T-shirts made for all the players and coaches: gold shirts with black writing, player or coach's jersey number on the left sleeve, *SENIOR WEEKEND 2006* on the left chest, and *A Merry Band of Coxmen* the back of every shirt—an inside joke from the movie *Wedding Crashers*, which we'd watched on the bus on some of our trips.

I spent $800 of my own money on the T-shirts—around 70 percent of what I had earned the entire season as a broadcaster. It was money I couldn't afford to spend, but I felt it was important to put a charge into the players with a gift. If we could win the series against UT, it would give us a great chance to get a bid in the NCAA Tournament. We needed to show the NCAA that we were capable of beating another top-tier opponent like we had earlier in the season when we beat Florida. To wrestle a series from the Longhorns would be huge for us.

When I got to the ballpark for the first game of the UT series, I grabbed the cardboard box filled with more than forty T-shirts and raced to the dugout. I dropped the box at the end of the bench and immediately went up to the broadcast booth to grab the tape recorder for my pregame interviews, always recorded an hour before the game, saved, and inserted into the broadcast ten minutes before the first pitch of every game. The interview that day would be with Tony Vitello. He and I had not done a one-on-one interview the entire season; we had wanted to wait until an important time in the year to put our chemistry on the air.

I pulled Tony out of the bullpen and told him that it was time for us to do our pregame interview. I could tell he was fired up for the battle with Texas. We walked from the bullpen slowly down the left-field line, and I prepped him with the questions that I was going to ask on tape. When we got behind third base, in foul territory, I turned on the tape recorder.

"Our pregame guest today is Missouri pitching coach Tony Vitello. Coach, can you tell me what you anticipate when the Tigers and the Longhorns go at each other in this important three-game set?"

"Well, Mike, I think we are just going to kick the fuck out of these guys!"

I looked at him for a moment and then erupted in laughter. He had seen me do dozens of pregame interviews and had been patiently waiting all season to drop that joke. We laughed hysterically for a good five minutes and slapped high fives before I could start the interview over again.

"Coach, what do you think about this weekend series with the Longhorns?"

"I think we are going to have our hands full, Mike. We will need to play our best baseball to win this series."

* * *

We won game one of the series with a lights-out pitching performance from Scherzer; he was unhittable and nasty. He had a major-league arm even in college, and college hitters had no chance against him. After the game, Tony and I were jacked up. We had dinner and a few drinks at Shakespeare's Pizza, and then we went back to Tony's. I stayed up all night watching television. My mania was now full blown.

I left Tony's at six the next morning and went to practice at the short-game area at Eagle Knoll, where I played for about four hours and then went straight to the ballpark. We won game two 8–5 and were one win from a sweep. We were all fired up after the second victory against the Longhorns. That night, I went out and I got piss drunk. I started with beers at dinner and then went bar hopping all over Columbia. Beers turned into shots, which turned to whiskey drinks, and before I knew it, I blacked out.

I woke up outside a church, on the outskirts of town. There were statues of Mary and Jesus near the ten-foot-tall mahogany doors at the top of the steps. I had no idea where I was or how I had gotten there, much less where Tony was. Fortunately, there was a small amount of battery power left in my cell phone, and I was able to call Paul Kruger, our team's student manager. He tracked me down around 5:45 a.m.

Paul got me safely back to Tony's house, where I collapsed onto the couch and passed out. But I didn't sleep long. Tony woke me up around eight o'clock, when he left for the ballpark. I stayed on the couch until nine when I decided, of all things, to clean the upstairs bathroom in Tony's house. I had taken a shower in there and noticed it was a mess, the dirty work of three guys in their midtwenties who hadn't cleaned it in months. It looked like bottles of toothpaste and shampoo had thrown up all over the floor. The tub looked like blacktop. It was disgusting.

I turned up the CD player and got to work. I wiped the counter, scrubbed the tub, shined all the chrome on the faucets, washed and dried the rugs, bleached the toilet. The room started out looking like a frat house bathroom and wound up looking like it belonged in a suite at the Ritz-Carlton. I even lit candles when I finished. My mania cleaned that room.

When I finished my spring-cleaning project, it was time for me to get to the ballpark. I was there about an hour and a half before the first pitch. I came up with the brilliant idea of getting inside the heads of the Texas players.

I was wearing my customary attire to broadcast a Tiger game: a black ball cap with a giant gold M, a black collared shirt with a gold M on the left breast, and mirrored Oakley sunglasses. I hadn't shaved in days, so I had a grizzly beard. I grabbed a broom from Tony's office and made my way to the Texas dugout. I walked down the stairs of the dugout and began sweeping the stairs and the floor, looking directly at the handful of Longhorn players who were there preparing for the game. I was blatantly taunting the players that they were going to get swept. After a few minutes, I chucked the broom into the corner of the dugout and retreated to Tony's office, grabbed a bottle of water, and went upstairs to the broadcast booth.

I couldn't sit still during the pregame. I was in and out of my chair in the booth a dozen times in five minutes. Tex had no clue what he was in for.

At this point in the season, I had already called more than fifty games. I had made a conscious effort in all of those games to be positive toward all the players, on both teams. But my ripening mania changed my approach in this final game with Texas.

Every time a Texas batter came to the plate, I declared that they had no chance to hit our pitching. I repeatedly said, "This guy is nothing." My mania and all the alcohol from the night before were creating a rage that made me verbally abusive to each and every Longhorn player, not just hitters. "There was a reason this guy wasn't their number-one starter," I said about their pitcher. "He's a chump!"

The more I ripped on Texas, the more runs the Tigers scored. The voodoo was working, and I cursed the opposition with my commentary. When I was manic and things were going my way, I continued whatever behavior I was doing without any regard for anyone else. Bipolar disorder makes you extremely selfish.

Tex put up with it—probably because he didn't know what to do—until the fifth inning, when he kicked me out of the booth to cool off. I deserved it.

He let me come back into the booth after an inning. I repeatedly apologized to him for my actions during a break in the broadcast and was better for the final three innings of the game.

As soon as the game was over (we swept the Longhorns), I raced down to the field, took care of my postgame interview with Coach Jamieson, and then headed for the parking lot; I had a Gateway Section event the next day. I went to my car, turned the Counting Crows on again as loud as the volume would go, and sped back to St. Louis.

* * *

The Section tournament the next day was at Annbriar Golf Course, in Waterloo, Illinois, which is about forty minutes from St. Louis. With mania at its peak, I didn't get a wink of sleep the night before. I had played Annbriar at least twenty-five times and had driven myself there each and every time. But I never made it to the course that day.

I got turned around in a neighborhood about twenty minutes from the course and lost all directional bearings. I circled the neighborhood for forty minutes, seeing the same houses, the same Mizzou flag on one of them, getting more and more frustrated and paranoid as the minutes passed. I was going to be late for my tee time. I was also slowly losing my mind into a dangerous abyss.

After circling the neighborhood too many times to count, I finally found a street that got me out of the labyrinth. It was now past my tee time, but I had already forgotten about that and just wanted to drive home. But my mind was moving too fast for any sort of reasonable thought. When I made it back onto the main highway, running through the farmland of Southern Illinois, my Honda ran out of gas.

My mind began playing serious tricks on me when my car ran out of fuel. I started to believe that it was trying to injure me. As I sat in the car, I felt like the car was closing in on me, because I was embarrassed about running out of gas, so I just sat on the side of the highway for thirty minutes trying over and over to start the car. If the definition of insanity is repeating the same action and hoping for a different result, I was totally I-N-S-A-N-E.

Finally, I decided to push the car. So I put it in neutral, got out, and began pushing the car down the shoulder. Cars flew past me. I was dressed in pressed khaki trousers and a royal blue and white striped polo shirt, sweating profusely in the eighty-five-degree heat, slowly pushing my Honda down the road with every ounce of strength that I had. I began to feel like the car was going to kill me, like it was out to get me. So, I decided I would kill the car before it killed me.

I stopped pushing and popped the trunk. I remembered that Pilk had won a Louisville Slugger baseball bat in a charity golf scramble and had left it in my car. I grabbed the bat and went to work on the car, channeling my favorite MLB hitters. I smashed in the door to the gas tank with my best Mark McGwire home run swing. Then I switched it up and connected again in the area of the gas tank with another big swing. Next I moved to the driver-side door, which was still open, and went Jose Canseco with the biggest swing I had in me to shatter the window. I took a few quick hits on the interior of the driver-side door that destroyed the window buttons and the power locks.

Take that, motherfucker!

Traffic continued to pass me as I destroyed the car. I exploded the windshield like a lumberjack chopping wood, sending glass flying everywhere. My forearms were bleeding from the glass shards, but I didn't care. I moved to the passenger side, smashing both windows and doors. It must have been quite a sight for anyone driving by to see a man taking apart his car with a baseball bat while dressed in perfectly ironed clothing.

I felt better after killing the car. I knew it couldn't come after me, because it was out of fuel and destroyed, but I wanted to get as far away from it as possible. I needed to grab a few items to bring with me, so I went back to the open trunk and grabbed my gym bag and the driver from my golf bag. I left the rest of my clubs in the trunk. There was some sort of underlying importance that made me believe that I only needed that one club to use as a weapon while I was on foot. I strapped the gym bag on like a backpack, held the driver in my right hand like a spear, and jogged away from the scene.

I was running in between the northbound and southbound interstate lanes in grass that was two feet tall. It was a hot and sticky day in May, and I was drenched in sweat. I had covered about a mile when I came across a driving range just off the interstate. It looked like an oasis, and I raced toward it. I crossed the southbound lane of the highway, tossed my gym bag and my trusty Bridgestone driver over the barbed wire fence, then scaled it, further cutting up my arms in the process. I flipped over the fence head first, landing on my back. There was a small clubhouse to my left, and at the far right side of the driving range, there was a chipping green. I headed to the green, holding my gym bag like a briefcase and resting my driver on my shoulder. There was no one else on the driving range. I was all alone.

When I got to the chipping green, I pulled a pair of black athletic shorts out of my gym bag, took off my golf trousers, and put on the shorts. I grabbed a white T-shirt from the bag and substituted my golf shirt for the plain white tee. I took off my shoes but kept on my black dress socks. I found a few stray range balls and began to hit.

The owner of the driving range saw me through the window, hitting balls in my shorts, T-shirt, black socks, and no shoes. A police car showed up in the parking lot not long after. I walked toward the police car with my driver in hand. When the cop asked me how I got to the driving range—the only car in the parking lot belonged to the owner—I answered with a standard manic lie. I said I had been dropped off at the range. He told me that the owner wanted me off his property and that he would give me a ride where I needed to go.

I didn't argue because I was interested in seeing where this journey would take me next.

I ran back to the chipping green to grab my gym bag and tennis shoes before getting into the police car. I wasn't handcuffed and the cop was very cordial. I even rode in the front seat with him. I was so completely out of my mind that I didn't even ask him where we were going; I just sat next to him and carried on pleasant conversation. Finally, we reached our destination, the Columbia Police Department. I wasn't alarmed. I knew I hadn't done anything against the law, and even if they locked me up, in my current mind-set, I didn't care. I was ready to face any situation.

In my most manic state, I can only think of the present moment. If only I could duplicate that ability on the golf course. The mania does not allow me to look back or forward—that's one of the reasons it is so difficult for me to notice when I am in the middle of a manic episode. If I were able to reflect on my past, maybe I could recall some experience that would allow me to fight off the mania. Unfortunately, it doesn't work that way.

I had left my wallet in my car, so I didn't have any ID on me. But I told them my real name and my real address. They kept me in the front lobby of the police station while they checked out my information. I stood up and sat down every other minute while watching a small television and practicing correct golf posture with my driver, which—for some reason—they had allowed me to keep. I waited in the lobby for what seemed like eternity but was actually only an hour. The police officer who had given me a ride came into the lobby to tell me that they wouldn't be charging me with anything. He told me that a taxi was on its way to pick me up and take me home.

* * *

I tried to make conversation with the cabbie, but he didn't want any of it. When we pulled into the parking lot at Pilk's apartment, I told the driver that I had to run inside and grab my checkbook so I could pay him. He wasn't happy about accepting a check, but my wallet was still on the side of the road in Illinois, so I promised that the tip would be worthwhile. He agreed, and I cut him a hot check for $150 for a $70 fare, made out to him rather than the cab company. I was doing it again, giving away money that I didn't have. The cabbie drove away happy, leaving me to embark on a manic romp around Pilk's apartment.

Things were about to get strange again, but I only realized that in retrospect; at the time, I thought all my actions were normal.

I put on that same Counting Crows CD at full blast in the kitchen and I propped open the door to the deck. I was ready for more manic cleaning.

The cleaning went on for a couple of hours. After I finished, I felt as if the apartment needed a facelift. I took picture frames from the third floor and exchanged them with frames on the main floor. I moved furniture around. I stood on dining chairs and disconnected light fixtures that looked evil to me. Everything made sense at the time. All the adjustments were necessary to keep Pilk and me safe.

I went down to the basement and made more adjustments. I took an old broken computer screen and keyboard and put both of them into the dryer. I found some of Pilk's old football gear and put on a helmet, which I kept on when I went to the convenience store for a bottle of water. It is safe to say that I was out of my mind, but all these moves seemed calculated and smart in the moment.

When I got back to the apartment after my trip to the convenience store, I was determined to attack the voodoo doll that was still hanging in my closet. The music blared at full volume.

I brought the voodoo doll into the kitchen, where I got out the cutting board. I believed that the doll was Satan trapped in Ken's plastic body, and I was going to kill him in a gruesome fashion and make him feel excruciating pain. I put on a pair of winter gloves to perform the dismemberment. I began by cutting off the doll's legs, then his arms, and then his head—the pieces spread out carefully on the cutting board.

I went upstairs and grabbed a handful of pushpins from my room. I then inserted them all over the doll's torso, intending to inflict the ultimate pain on Satan. I filled a Tupperware container with a concoction of barbecue sauce, mustard, and mayonnaise. Since I absolutely hate mayonnaise, this was the worst fate I could imagine. I dropped the doll's head into the Tupperware container in the hopes of drowning Satan in condiments.

I had to be very thorough in my execution. I sealed the container and put it in the freezer. Then I went outside and placed the legs and torso on the barbecue grill and doused them in lighter fluid. I lit them on fire and watched them burn. I felt relieved, like I had done a great justice for mankind.

I closed the grill but I wasn't finished. The head was still in the freezer; I waited for about an hour before removing it and adding it to the other pieces, now charred black on the barbecue grill. I made the switch. After I put the head on the grill, I put the legs, arms, and torso into the Tupperware container and shook the pinkish sludge. I put the container back in the freezer and closed the grill. My job was complete. I had murdered Satan.

I cleaned up the kitchen so Pilk wouldn't know what I had done, but it was all too obvious that I wasn't in my right mind when he got home from work. He walked into the apartment to find new pictures and posters on the walls. He saw the detached light fixtures and found the computer screen and keyboard in the dryer. He was alarmed. He called Nick.

Nick Sansone was the only person who could shake any sense into me. He had seen what bipolar disorder had done to me over the years and had always been there when I needed him. Pilk knew about some of my issues but had never experienced them up close and personal. He knew that Nick was more familiar with my situation.

Nick dropped what he was doing and came over right away. I was up in my room and had no idea that he was coming, but I caught a glimpse of him as he approached the front door. I was excited to see him, one of my best friends from childhood. He came upstairs and we met at my doorway.

I could tell by the look on his face that he wasn't happy. He grabbed me by the throat and shoved me up against the door. Nick is not a guy you want to mess with; he is naturally strong and knows how to fight. He's the guy who takes kickboxing classes for fun. I was scared by Nick's attempt at tough love.

"You are coming with me right now, or I am going to knock your head off," he said in a slow, quiet tone that put fear into every part of me. I trusted Nick more than anyone—I still do—so I didn't even question him. We got in his car and the conversation returned to a regular tone. He knew that if he got me in the car, he could get me to the hospital.

* * *

Nick took me to Barnes–Jewish Hospital. My dad was there to meet us when we arrived in the emergency room. I have now had five trips to the Barnes emergency room, and every single one has been exactly the same: You are admitted in the main waiting room and then escorted to a small holding cell in the belly of the hospital. The cell is just that: eight feet by eight feet, white floor, white walls, twin mattress—but no box spring—on the floor, and a camera watching your every move. It's a scary and lonely room, something right out of the movie *12 Monkeys*.

You can leave the cell only to use the bathroom. After a couple of hours, you're pushed through the bowels of the hospital in a wheelchair, back up to the friendly confines of the fifteenth floor. I had learned during my first stay on fifteen that if I kept my mouth shut and was on my best behavior, I'd be released in just a few days. So, I acted the part and took my meds for four days, expecting to be back on the loose in no time.

Pilk didn't want me to move back into the apartment after the episode. I can't really blame him. If you're not familiar with bipolar disorder and what it can cause people to do, it can be intimidating and completely unnerving.

* * *

My dad met me when I was released. I hopped into the car as if I had just gotten out of school and he was driving car pool. He told me how important it was that I take my medicine. He also broke the news that I wasn't welcome back at Pilk's place and that I'd been fired from the baseball team. I was homeless, carless, and had lost my dream job. I was not in a good spot, but I was happy to be out. In retrospect, I should have stayed on fifteen awhile longer. I believe my dad knew that, too, but my happiness clouded his judgment. He always wanted what was best for me and to see me happy. I imagine parents must often struggle to balance a child's welfare and their happiness. My ability to play the role of improving patient sped my release and fooled my parents and the doctors into thinking I was fit to be discharged.

I chose to take my unemployment and homelessness as a challenge: I would find a place to live and a way to get around on my own. The manic brain believes that it can do everything by itself. It doesn't understand that no one can function without help. Pride and ego will do that to you.

I decided to move into my safe haven, the Missouri Athletic Club, which has three floors of hotel rooms. To fund my new lifestyle, I applied for a new credit card with a high limit and an even higher APR.

I borrowed my dad's car to pick up my belongings from Pilk's. When I returned the car, I told my parents I was going to stay with an obscure high school friend who I was sure they didn't know. I was only at the club for a few days before things began to get strange again.

* * *

I needed to get my hands on a car since I had killed mine. St. Louis is a city in which you drive everywhere. I could easily cover more than a hundred miles in a single day around the Gateway City, just living my everyday life. So, I checked the phone book for a dealership that would lease me a car. The first name I found was Ed Napleton Honda. Perfect. I had gone to college with Ed Napleton, Jr., and figured I could drop his name while talking to the salesman and get a good deal.

After making the thirty-five-mile trip to the dealership by taxi, I gave the salesman my spiel about my good friend Ed, Jr., who had suggested I come see what kind of deal I could get. After two hours of banter, test drives, and paperwork, I drove off the lot with my new ride.

The first night that I had my new car, I got pulled over on my way to

Harpo's, Matt Ratz's bar in the western suburbs. The cop pulled me over, literally in the parking lot at Harpo's, for doing seventy in a forty-five-mile-per-hour zone. I was a complete asshole to the police officer as he put me through the series of sobriety tests, knowing that he couldn't charge me for a DUI. I hadn't had a drop of alcohol since getting out of the hospital, though I would have if I hadn't been broke.

"Hey copper, do you like bacon? I love bacon," I taunted him, my wild eyes glaring.

He interpreted my manic taunting as my being under the influence of some substance, so he took me to the Chesterfield Police Department. I sat in a cell for about thirty minutes before he came in and told me I would have to take a breathalyzer test.

"Let's do it!" I knew my system was clean and had already called a lawyer, so I wanted to watch this guy's reaction. Sure enough, the result was 0.0 blood alcohol level.

"That can't be right." He said. "We are going to try it again."

The look of disbelief on his face when the 0.0 popped up again was priceless, and I mocked him for it. I took the test one more time—0.0 again. The cop was pissed. He had nothing to hold me on. The cop called my lawyer, who told him that I was bipolar. So, instead of releasing me, the Chesterfield Police escorted me back to Barnes–Jewish Hospital, where they turned me over to the emergency room staff.

I was examined and given a blood test for illegal drugs, which also came up clean. After just an hour in the hospital, I was released. I walked out of the emergency room, found a taxi, and went back to the Missouri Athletic Club around two o'clock in the morning.

I tried to sleep, but there was no chance of me settling down enough. At four o'clock, I went down to the fitness floor and worked out for an hour. I dashed from the abdominal machine to the bench press to the rowing machine and finally to the pool for frantic laps, sprinting freestyle while trying to formulate a plan to get my car out of the impound lot. I went back to my room and tried to watch TV but couldn't sit in one position for longer than a few minutes. I counted the minutes until I could call to find my car.

While I killed time, I nearly killed myself in my hotel room. I took one of my shoelaces and wrapped it around my neck. I tightened the shoelace until my face was as red as ketchup in the bathroom mirror. It was almost as if my bipolar mind was tightening the lace around my neck and my conscious brain was fending off the disorder and loosening the lace so I could breathe again. My bipolar mind was daring me to make the choice to stay alive. I would tighten it, then loosen. Tighten, then loosen. I'm not sure how long it went on but I recall thinking that I may die looking in that mirror. But I chose to live.

At nine o'clock, I called a cab to pick me up at the club. The Chesterfield Police Department told me that my car was impounded at a Valley Park junkyard. It would cost me $250 to get it out. I cashed another hot check at the front desk of the club for $350 to pay for the cab ride and cover the fee to free my car. The cab ride cost $30, but I gave the cab driver $100— giving money away again.

I got out of the cab at a red light at a very busy intersection, cars whipping by at fifty miles per hour, a few of them missing me by inches. The gusts of wind from the passing cars nearly knocked me into traffic. I narrowly avoided being killed on my way to the lot.

I had been manically texting Ratz during the cab ride to meet me for lunch, as the impound lot was near his house. Instead of Ratz, Nick showed up to get me. My friends kept a call ring going when they knew I was manic so they could find me when I put myself in danger. Ratz, Nick, Michael Eveler, Ryan Schuette, and my old college roommate Patrick Madigan all reported to each other when I contacted any of them. Ratz could tell from my rapid texts that I was not well, so he called Eveler, and Eveler called Nick.

Nick saved my life by coming to get me that day.

While I walked to the impound lot, I noticed a cellular phone store in a commercial real estate property. I hadn't paid my cell phone bill in a couple of months and feared it could be turned off at any moment, so I went in and bought a new phone with my new credit card. I would figure out later how to pay the bill; my manic brain wasn't capable of forward thinking. When I walked out of the cell phone store, Nick was waiting for me. I was happy to see him. It never occurred to me why he would be there; I was just excited to see a familiar face.

"You're coming with me to the hospital right now."

"The fuck I am!" My excitement had turned to defiance in an instant. It was the first time I had ever raised my voice at Nick.

He didn't respond, just tackled me to the cement like he was Lawrence Taylor sacking a helpless quarterback behind the line of scrimmage.

As my best friend was pinning me down on the sidewalk, it finally hit me that something was very wrong. I trusted Nick. He would take a bullet to save my life. He would never tackle me in a parking lot unless it was absolutely necessary.

Once he got me in the car, his tone changed back to my old friend.

"Mike, I have to take you to the hospital so they can check you out." He told me in a relaxed tone.

"Alright, man. If that is what you think needs to happen, let's go." His voice put me at ease, but I knew I was heading toward an extended stay at Barnes.

* * *

My dad was at the emergency entrance when we arrived. It was back to the fifteenth floor at Barnes–Jewish Hospital, my manic home away from home. I felt as though I had let my doctors and the nurses down, because I was already back. And yet I was also pissed. I clenched my fists and ground my teeth as I walked up and down the familiar hallway. I felt like everyone in the world was against me, like Nick and my dad were responsible for me winding up in the hospital again.

Another challenge of the manic brain is that it doesn't want any help from anyone. It believes that it is infallible. I was a complete mess, and the hospital was the best place for me, but I couldn't help feeling angry about the confinement.

As a patient on fifteen, you enjoy a small amount of freedom. You can watch television and movies in the living room; you can use any of the phones whenever you like; and during certain times of the day, you can use the rec room and play pool or Ping-Pong, and even get on the Internet. When a patient is participating in their own recovery, the floor is a conducive environment.

I needed to get in touch with Hope. I hadn't talked to her in four or five days. She still didn't know about my bipolar issues, and I was in love with her and had to speak to her as soon as possible. I called her at the restaurant where she was working nights at the time. She wasn't there the first time I called, or the second or the third. On the fourth try, I got into a verbal altercation with the bartender who answered the phone.

"Is Hope working tonight?" I inquired.

"She is. Can I tell her who is calling?"

"This is her boyfriend. Go get her right now," I demanded. I am very good at barking orders at people when I am in a manic state.

"Excuse me?"

"I need to speak to her immediately. Go get her."

"I will tell her you called, but she is busy and can't take any calls right now."

I hung up on him.

And then, like the mania that was eating my mind, a feeling of loneliness drenched my heart.

My parents didn't want to talk to me, and my friends were disappointed in me for not taking my medication. I didn't get out of bed during the first three days of this hospitalization. I mistreated every doctor and nurse who was trying to help me, responding to their questions with short, one-word answers.

"Mr. Wellington, are you awake?" they asked.

"No!" I would yell and turn over in my bed.

I didn't attend any of the group therapy sessions. I never watched any TV or used the rec room. I hid in my self-created cocoon of victimization, playing the *Why me?* game in my head. I was in complete denial about needing to be in the hospital.

On the fourth day, I finally got in touch with Hope.

"Hope, I am in Barnes Hospital. My parents put me in here because they don't think I am healthy, but they don't know what they are talking about." I explained to her.

She was hesitant to visit me in the hospital but changed her mind after Nick visited her at the hair salon. Nick was always saving the day, even from behind the scenes. He knew how much I liked her and felt that she was the only person who could get through to me at the time.

* * *

Visiting hours on the floor are only one hour a night, from 7:00 to 8:00.

When Hope arrived to visit me, I was flabbergasted. I hadn't thought I would see her again after the phone conversation I had had with her coworker at the restaurant and, in that moment, I had never felt more love for a woman in my life. I was in shock that she had actually come to see me. She looked like a movie star with her short and trendy blonde hair. She was wearing a red V-neck blouse that would have made Jessica Simpson jealous, and a pair of black pants that looked both professional and sexy.

Hope took life head-on, and I respect her so much for that trait. I was in the mental hospital, the psych ward, the loony bin, where they keep the straightjackets, and she had come to see me. We sat down at a table in the cafeteria. It felt like she was coming to visit me in jail, just without the glass divider separating us.

I told her the details of my struggle with bipolar disorder and explained that this wasn't the first time I had been hospitalized. She didn't judge me; she just listened. I tried to fit as many words into the hour as I could, but it went by so quickly that it felt like ten minutes. When visiting hours were over, she told me she would return, and I went to bed that night with an ear-to-ear grin.

* * *

By morning, I had slipped back into surly bipolar mode. I had no idea how long I would be in the hospital, and I was ready for some answers. Dr. Cloninger was out of the country and wouldn't return for another eight days or so. I trusted him and was not comfortable talking to the other doctors, which impeded my recovery progress.

I got on the phone again. I only knew a few numbers by heart, this being the age of the cell phone and the digital contact list. One of those numbers was Nick's. I called him and we had it out. I was angry, but he put me in my place.

"Why the fuck am I in here, and why would you help put me in here?" I barked at him.

"You need to be in there until you start taking your medicine every day."

"What are you—my parents?"

"You're lucky your dad is such a nice man, because if you were my son, I would have beaten the living shit out of you by now. Do what the doctors are telling you to do and then you will get out. If you don't listen, you will be in there for a while."

The conversation just frustrated me further, so I hung up. My world had completely caved in: My best friend wanted to kick my ass, my family wouldn't talk to me, and I was trapped indoors—away from golf—on a beautiful June day. Coincidentally, one window on fifteen overlooks the golf course at Forest Park. Catching a glimpse of the course was salt in the wound. I paced up and down the main hallway, trying to figure out a way to escape. My blood boiled as I walked from my bedroom out to the phone booths in the cafeteria area.

Boredom and anger are about the worst combination for the bipolar manic mind. I blamed others for my being in the hospital. I wasn't mature or mentally stable enough to own the situation that I had put myself into. I blamed my mom for no real reason. Although the hospital staff had been giving me the proper medication every night before bed, my mind had not yet returned to any form of reasonable thinking during the five days I had been there. The lingering traces of mania and my anger at the situation made me frantic for attention, so I took it upon myself to make my mom feel the effects of my anger.

I sat in one of the phone booths with a phone book and looked up the number to the stationery shop where my mom worked. I hung up when someone answered, then immediately called back and hung up again. I did it over and over. It got to the point where no one would answer the phone, so I just let it ring and ring and ring. I let the phone ring for a ten full minutes at a time and then stopped for a minute before starting up again, for an hour. I was acting like a four-year-old having a tantrum.

My mom finally realized it was me. She called the hospital, which had one of the nurses come over to my phone booth and stop me. I was banned from using the phone for the rest of the day.

* * *

Hope came back that night. I was beginning to persuade her that my parents and friends were all bad people who were against me for petty reasons. In actuality, I was the petty one. Hope knew I wasn't a big fan of the hospital food, and she was so thoughtful that she always brought food with her. Our relationship was getting stronger every day; we sat together in the hospital, talking over dinner every night, and learned more and more about each other. I was ten days into my stay, and the medications were beginning to stabilize my moods; Hope was also a calming influence. That is when my best friends decided to make their move to help me along.

Over a three-day stretch, I was visited by ten people who all had the best intentions. Nick came by himself around dinnertime, with an extra-large sausage and pepperoni pizza from Imo's. Our last conversation had been ugly, but Nick never gave up on me. When I saw him this time, we both smiled and laughed, with sheepish grins because we knew who I truly was. Nick's visit was a reminder for me of how important it was that I take my medication when I got out of the hospital. He made it clear that the medicine was the ingredient my body needed to live the right way.

The next day, I was visited by four close friends that used the opportunity as part of a mini-intervention. Michael Eveler was, of course, my best friend from childhood; Dan Heath was my high school golf teammate, and I had known him since the eighth grade; Mike Fleming was a high school basketball teammate and partner in crime both in high school and in college; and Pilk was my former roommate. I was surprised that Pilk came to see me in the hospital. He had no experience with bipolar disorder, and after what I had done to his apartment, he could have easily turned his back on me. The other guys had helped me through other manic spells in the past. They were all clear and concise in the reason for their visit.

"Michael, you know how important it is that you take this medicine, right?" I hated hearing Eveler talk to me like I was a toddler.

"Yes, Eveler. I have been taking it every day in here." I told him as I rolled my eyes.

"Wells, this is a serious deal. Look where you are. This is something you need to take seriously." Fleming chimed in when he saw me roll my eyes.

"Flems, I know I need to take it, and I am going to take it. I don't want to be in here anymore. The food sucks here." No one thought that was funny. "Pilk, I am really sorry about turning your apartment upside down."

"Do you remember any of that?" He questioned with seriousness.

"Yeah, I remember it all. This bipolar thing doesn't black you out like booze does, just makes you do things you wouldn't normally do." I told him.

"Michael, how was your golf game before you came into the hospital?" Heath asked, trying to lighten the mood. He was an avid Ben Hogan fan, and we always talked golf with each other.

They were a good team. They had to get into my head and make sure that I knew how important it was that I take my medicine. They told me to look where I was and challenged me to get healthy and get out of there. They were firm; it wasn't the most pleasant conversation, but I needed it. I am forever grateful that they all came to see me; their persistence was much appreciated.

The following day, I was hit with another mini-intervention by four more of my close friends. Nick brought a group of guys with him whose opinions I valued greatly: Dan Finney was there—our friendship went all the way back to kindergarten—and Ryan Schuette came with them, even though I had attacked him a year earlier at the concert. My bipolar behavior had put a major strain on our friendship, but Schuette knew how important it was that he be there to add to the group. Patrick Madigan was my high school golf partner and college roommate; he had driven three-hours from Osage Beach, Missouri, to be part of the intervention.

"Wells, you need to take the lithium. It's that simple." Madigan started the conversation while we sat at a round table.

Four more of my best friends with the same message: *Take the medicine, Michael.*

This group was even more straightforward in their approach. Nick was not the nice guy who had brought me pizza two days earlier. He made it known that if I didn't get on board with taking my medicine he couldn't continue our friendship.

"Mike, this needs to be your number-one priority," Nick said, in a serious tone. "It needs to be ahead of golf, ahead of your broadcasting job. If you don't focus on taking the lithium, I don't want to be around you."

Finney was equally firm. He reminded me of how, three years earlier,

I had helped him with his own bipolar struggles and how his life had improved tenfold since accepting his medicine as a daily requirement.

"Mike, you know I know how you feel," he said. "Take the medicine. It's working for me, and it can work for you." Finney always had simple and clear advice.

"Well, Dan, if you can do it, then I can do it too." I announced.

"Wells, I love ya, man. Get better and we will see you when you get out of here," Schuette said before leaving the floor.

I began to look at things differently. My friends meant everything to me. At twenty-eight, I was closer to my friends than I was to my family. I wouldn't have listened to my parents, but my friends got through to me. It was an epiphany that I wish had come much earlier—but better late than never.

My last visitor that week was Jay Eveler, Michael's father. Jay is like a second father to me, and we had a great relationship. I respect him and his opinions. He took a different approach with his meeting. He never once mentioned the medication. He had brought a list with him of athletes, actors, musicians, and business moguls who all had been diagnosed with bipolar disorder. When I looked at the list, there were people on it that I greatly admired; people like Matt Cameron, Dick Cavett, Rosemary Clooney, Robert Downey, Jr., Richard Dreyfuss, Carrie Fisher, Mel Gibson, Linda Hamilton, Frank Sinatra, and Ted Turner had all been diagnosed with bipolar disorder. They all had successful lives and careers. But on the flip side, Kurt Cobain was bipolar, which surely played a role in his suicide.

In addition to sharing the list of names, Jay also brought me up to date with my Missouri Tiger baseball team. I hadn't been with them for almost two weeks, and they were on a roll, playing hard for me. One of the blessings of my disorder is that, I believe, it helped them refocus and win the regional and move on to the super regional that would be played in Malibu, California. It stung to know I wouldn't be able to play my role for the team, but they were on their way to competing at the highest level, in one of the most beautiful places in our country—and I was stuck on the fifteenth floor of a hospital. Missing that trip—the time with Vitello and supporting the team—is one thing that the disorder has robbed from me that still brings tears to my eyes and pisses me off.

Jay's tactic with the list helped me to see that there are very successful and creative people who live with bipolar disorder all over the world but also to be aware that bipolar disorder can kill too. Jay promised to keep me up to date on my Tigers as they moved forward into the super regional.

My mind was beginning to look at things differently. Realizing that I was missing the trip with the team was an enormous wake-up call; it made me feel embarrassed because I had left my team hanging.

* * *

Hope was still visiting me every night, and I was getting better, but the beautiful blue skies and sunny weather outside was driving me bananas: I couldn't play golf, and it was getting to me. I had been in the hospital for eleven days when Dr. Cloninger returned from his trip abroad. When I finally got to sit down with him, I immediately felt more secure that I would be getting out soon. The medication had taken effect, but Dr. Cloninger told me I would be caged another five days or so; I felt relieved to finally have a target release date. But even though the meds were stabilizing my mood, I still wasn't playing golf.

My friends' visits had helped, but instead of participating in group therapy sessions, socializing in the rec room, or meeting with doctors (other than Dr. Cloninger), I did the bare minimum. I thought I was above all of it. I took the medicine that was fed to me every night, but that was it. Unfortunately, that's not how things work on fifteen. The doctors don't take you seriously until it is obvious that you are going out of your way to get better. I was keeping to myself each day by staying in my room and counting the hours until Dr. Cloninger would set me free.

During all this time in the hospital, I had had very little contact with my parents. I was still angry with them and made no attempt to touch base with them. Except for the crazy phone calls to my mom's office. I took out most of my frustration on them. It is really amazing how the negative bipolar mind always attacks the people who care about you the most. I listened to Hope and all my friends who came to see me in the hospital, but I didn't listen to a word from my parents; my mom avoided visiting altogether, and the few times that my dad came, I berated him so badly that he left after just a few minutes. At the time, I wasn't aware of my anger, and I had no chance or desire to control it.

One of the key elements in changing my perspective during this hospital stay was my sister, Amy, who at the time lived in Charlotte, North Carolina. While my family and friends in St. Louis were unhappy with me because of my behavior and my attitude, my sister was removed from all of that negative energy. She and I were able to have rational conversations over the phone while I was in the hospital.

Because Amy lived elsewhere, she helped me begin to shift my thought process to becoming more aware of my illness. Just more proof that therapy doesn't have to be with a doctor or mental health professional. Therapy can happen with anyone you trust. That "brother-sister" bond I share with Amy gave me the trust to listen to her when I wouldn't listen to anyone else. She helped turn the tide for me in the right direction.

My parents, meanwhile, were working behind the scenes for my benefit. They felt like I needed to be in the hospital for an even longer period. They were getting reports from the doctors and nurses that I was not taking advantage of the daily activities provided, which would aid in my recovery. I was just biding my time, being selfish and standoffish when the doctors and social workers would approach me to join group therapy sessions. I would either park myself in my room or hole up in a phone booth and call Hope constantly.

My parents filed a notice of commitment with the Circuit Attorney's Office of St. Louis to hold me for an additional thirty days in the hospital. I found out about the filing when a lawyer showed up to help plan my defense. I was in shock to learn that I would be going to court against my parents. The lawyer really didn't make an effort to listen to me, didn't take anything I had to say seriously. Frankly, maybe he shouldn't have. I began to feel even angrier, knowing that my parents were trying to extend my incarceration. After sixteen days in Barnes–Jewish Hospital, I would face my parents in a court case to see how much longer I would be confined to the fifteenth floor. If I won the case, I would be out in only three more days; if my parents won, I would be released in no fewer than eleven days and no more than thirty.

Hope was so helpful during this time. She continued to see me every night at dinnertime, and she was baffled by my parents' desire for me to stay in the hospital. She hadn't met them and had only heard my side of the story. I was clinging to her for support, and she never wavered in being there when I needed her the most. She brought me a pair of gray slacks, black dress shoes, and a baby blue button-down shirt the day before the hearing, so I could dress appropriately for court.

The morning of the court case, I got dressed, and when I was ready to go, two paramedics came into my room with a stretcher and strapped me in with restraints over my chest, waist, and lower legs. They wheeled me down the hall to the elevators. We went down to the ambulance bay, where I got my first taste of fresh air in two weeks before being loaded into the back of the ambulance. The ride from the hospital to the Circuit Court Building made me highly anxious.

The ambulance pulled up to the front of the court building, where hundreds of people were on the street, going in and out of the revolving doors. The paramedics pulled me out of the ambulance and took me into the building. The elevator was full of strangers. It was easily the most awkward elevator ride of my life; I was wearing nice clothes and had a well-kept hairdo but was strapped to the gurney like Hannibal Lecter. I did my best not to look at anyone. As we got off the elevator, I was greeted by my parents' good friend and lawyer, Jerry Carmody. It was good to see a familiar face.

"Michael, how about you agree to the commitment? You will probably be in the hospital for only eleven more days?"

"I don't know, Jerry. I can't take it much longer in there. I want to see what happens in court."

After my brief conversation with Jerry, I was wheeled into the courtroom. It was something you would see in *Law and Order*: rows of benches from the back of the room to the front and then two tables within ten feet of the bench—one for the defense and one for the "prosecution." The room smelled like an old gymnasium filled with dust, and it was uncomfortably cold. The seal of the state of Missouri was painted above the judge's bench, and an American flag dangled over the door to the judge's chambers. The courtroom was empty except for lawyer, a bailiff standing near the window, and a handful of doctors waiting to affirm that I needed to stay longer.

The paramedics placed my stretcher at the table with my lawyer. I thought that my restraints would be taken off, but they stayed in place. The stretcher was tilted upward to face the bench. I have never felt more like a caged animal. The judge then entered the courtroom and took his seat behind the bench. He began by calling my dad to the stand. My dad talked about my history with bipolar disorder. He went on for ten minutes or so before I couldn't take it anymore. I whispered to my lawyer to get my dad down off the stand.

My dad was fighting back tears. My dad is a decent, hardworking, and honest man. It killed me to see him up there because of a situation that I had created. I had originally planned to take the stand in my defense, but after seeing my dad up there, I couldn't bring myself to oppose him, so I told my lawyer that I would just accept whatever sentence the judge came up with. He granted my parents' request to keep me detained for thirty more days, with the possibility of getting out early if I embraced the day-to-day activities of the hospital.

After the ruling, I just wanted to get out of there. When the paramedics came back to wheel me out, they turned me around to see not only my dad but both my mom and my brother in the back of the courtroom. I hadn't seen them yet, because I could only look from the gurney. When I was taken out of the courtroom, my dad put up his hand for a high five as I was going through the doors. That's Dad—ever positive, even when staring a bad situation right in the face. I slapped his hand as I passed by and recall realizing that I must have been really sick for it to get this far. That was a large turning point for me. I finally realized that I was not well and needed to work hard to get better.

The judge turned out to have a connection to my parents through a mutual friend and word got back to my mom that I was the only person in the history of his courtroom to ever show up in suit pants and a button-down shirt. Every other defendant had been clad in a hospital gown.

* * *

When I got back to fifteen, I knew it was time to participate in my recovery, which meant going to group sessions, spending time in the rec room, and talking in detail with the doctors in one-on-one meetings. The group meetings were helpful and aided in bringing me back to my usual self. Every day at 2:00 p.m., I checked my email and messaged my friends to tell them I was doing my best to get healthy and to get out of the hospital.

After checking my email each day, I had music therapy. Music is so powerful. There are songs and melodies that can make the hair on the back of your neck stand up. Those positive vibes can percolate through the body and stimulate the mind in a positive way. Music therapy is something that I still use today to naturally enhance my mood when I feel down. I recommend it not just to people who suffer from bipolar disorder but to anyone. Music can lead to a smile and in the fight against a mood disorder like mine, smiles never hurt.

* * *

I was finally trending in the right direction. But I didn't know how much longer I would be in the hospital. After eleven more days of quality improvement, I was allowed to leave the hospital and come back to the real world. Hope picked me up on the morning of my release; I had planned to stay with her for a little while so I could get my bearings.

The "incarceration" had done a number of positive things for me. I had now been completely sober and on my medication for a solid month. I finally knew that I would have to take my medicine every day without fail.

I moved in with Hope, but we didn't stay at her place for very long. She had confessed to me that her roommate's boyfriend had been physically abusive toward her and her roommate: slapping them around and pinning them up against the walls in the apartment. I don't stand for that type of shit. The boyfriend made an attempt to get me to fight him one night at their apartment; I didn't take the bait, but listening to his cocaine-induced threats made me realize that I needed to get Hope out of that situation. So we got a U-Haul truck, packed up all her things, and moved into a hotel room at the Missouri Athletic Club until we could find a new apartment. I made the mistake of getting another new credit card to pay for everything.

We found an apartment in a building in downtown St. Louis, but it turned out to be bad for both of us. The windows faced the wall of an adjacent building, and sunlight didn't get into our apartment until well after 1:00 p.m. every day. Living in relative darkness was driving me into a depressed state. My depression was leaking into Hope's outlook, and causing a major strain on our relationship. We had to get out of there.

Natural sunlight is an important tool in fighting depression. The vitamin D that the sun provides is essential for a positive mood.

My parents suggested that we move out of the city, and they found us a condominium. The new apartment had many windows and a lawn, with plenty of greenery surrounding the property. The new living space was much better for my mood. The closer a person with bipolar disorder can be to nature, the better.

* * *

Over the next few months, I spent my days teaching golf lessons and working on my golf game, and I still had a small hope to enter the 2006 Q-School. In August, I had a round that bolstered my confidence and made be seriously consider making another run at golf's holy grail. My good friend Jim Connors had come to St. Louis for a weekend of golf that included oppressively hot weather and great play by both of us. We played thirty-six holes on a Friday, and I made another hole in one at Westborough.

Jim and I came up on a foursome ahead of us that waived us through as they stood on the green and watched us play our tee shots into the fourth green. Jim hit first and played a solid shot that ended about fifteen feet from the hole. I stepped up and hit a chunky nine-iron shot, but my ball was headed right at the flag. It landed a foot to the right of the hole, spun directly left, rattled the flagstick and disappeared into the cup. The group on the green erupted with yells and screams. Jim and I laughed all the way to the green. Jim made his putt for birdie, and we moved on. It was a shot I will never forget.

After playing fifty-four holes on Friday and Saturday, we decided to play eighteen more on the Sunday, each day sweltering at more than 100 degrees. The radio hosts and television meteorologists had advised against being outside on a day like this, but we ignored them and played at

Stonewolf Golf Club in Fairview Heights. I birdied the first hole, which was my first birdie on my way to eight that day against no bogeys and a course record setting 64. It was a flawless round and stirred my interest in another stab at the Q-School.

In the end, I decided not to enter. It was actually a mature and healthy decision. I was six weeks removed from my longest stint in the hospital, and I just didn't think it was the right move at the time.

* * *

The new apartment wasn't the biggest living space, but Hope and I enjoyed it for a couple of months before things became difficult. Hope is totally selfless, and at the time, I was completely selfish; it was a bad combination. I had embraced the bachelor life for so long that I felt like the walls of the condo were caving in on me. I was living a married life, and I wasn't mature enough to handle it. We were spending lots of time together, but we were growing apart.

I told Hope that in the upcoming year, I would be on the road playing golf tournaments and wouldn't be in town a whole lot. She made it clear that she wanted a boyfriend who was present and not traveling all the time. By mid-December, we were finished. We sat on the floor of the condo and cried together, both realizing that we had to break up. The breakup was all on me; I knew that golf would take first priority and I would be back to traveling. Just before Christmas, Hope moved out. At the start of 2007, it was time for me to knock everything down, start over on my own, and build everything from the ground up. A fresh start with renewed focus was paramount.

THE FOURTEEN CLUBS

When I was feeling healthy, I stopped taking meds again, and that was the worst thing I could have done. The disorder had convinced me that I was free of it, but the bipolar mind (when unhealthy) can produce the strangest and most erratic behavior. I was only able to stay healthy when I trusted my doctor, my medication, and my routine. I also had incredible support from my friends and girlfriend during my hospital stay, and I couldn't have made it without them. Therapy and sleep—and not drinking—were what could have kept me sane.

6

THE ALBATROSS

It does not matter how many times you get knocked
down but how many times you get up.
—*Vince Lombardi*

I BEGAN 2007 focused solely on golf. My success to that point as a professional golfer had been rather limited, and my last hospital stay was quite lengthy. I needed to show some serious improvement in competition to keep the dream alive. I am sure a lot of people wondered whether I had any real talent on the golf course or whether my goal to play the PGA Tour was sheer fantasy. But I never stopped believing in myself, hospital gowns and all.

I decided that if I didn't prove myself worthy of continuing the pursuit of the tour by the end of the year, it would be time to go into another profession. I took my lithium religiously, every morning when I woke up, and my mind was getting stronger every day. I spent hours upon hours in the gym during the winter months doing intense workouts, with renewed focus. As the sweat poured out of me, I hoped the inner bipolar demons were getting exorcised too. I was supremely motivated to get my body in great shape to help improve my game.

The start of the golf season for me would be at the end of March; that's when I would begin competing again in the Gateway PGA Section. I spent the cold and snowy days of January, February, and the beginning of March hitting golf balls indoors at the Missouri Athletic Club and under the heaters at Tower Tee Golf Center in south St. Louis. I got good work in on my swing and my rhythm.

The Gateway Section would allow me to compete every week against talented players and also offered opportunities to make money with quality finishes. Regular Section events were held at great golf courses all over the metropolitan area; the first prize in many of those events was around $1,500, and the check for last place was around $100. It was stiff competition for not a lot of prize money, which put a greater emphasis on playing well.

That winter, my dad hired me to work as a courier again, and I spent a lot of time driving around St. Louis, making deliveries to all his printing clients. Sometimes I would move over 200 boxes in a day, all over St. Louis. I would start a day in south St. Louis and then head downtown to make a pickup. I would routinely travel forty minutes west of St. Louis and deliver boxes to his biggest client. I continued with my courier duties throughout the spring and summer as well. When the spring weather broke, I began teaching more and more golf lessons at Stonewolf. The courier job, teaching golf, practicing, and playing events were keeping me very busy, and that's a good recipe for well-being for a guy like me. The bipolar mind is so much more healthy when it is kept busy, with a regular routine, although not without proper medication. When the bipolar mind gets bored, that's when things can get out of whack; that's when the depressive side of the disorder can rear its ugly head. I spent every free minute I had either at the gym or working my ass off on my short game.

I wasn't going out very much, but I was far from sober. I drank on the weekends and on Wednesday and Thursday nights and during Monday Night Football . . . I drank a lot.

* * *

The golf season began slowly. I had a few decent finishes in Gateway events, making $200 here and $300 there. It wasn't a lot of money, but having paychecks show up in the mail was a great feeling, and it helped my confidence begin to blossom.

As I got to the middle of the summer, I was beginning to show signs of the potential that I always knew I had but had yet to put on full display. I tied for fourth at the Southern Illinois Open, shooting six under par for the twenty-seven-hole event. But my major breakthrough came at the Metropolitan Open at the Country Club of St. Albans's Lewis and Clark

Course in mid-July. The Met Open is a tournament that began in 2006 and has become the marquee open event in the state of Missouri. In fact, I filled out my entry form for the inaugural while on the fifteenth floor at Barnes Hospital. My dad had brought the form with him on a visit.

In the first round of the 2007 Met Open, I played a round of golf that I will always remember. USGA president Tom O'Toole's events always protect "old man par," which means that it is difficult to shoot low scores, because the course setup is stern; par is normally a great score at the Met Open. I played the first two rounds with two young prodigies, Mitchell Gregson and Scott Langely. Gregson ended up starring at Kansas State and won the Met Open in 2012. Langley was an all-American at the University of Illinois and is arguably the finest player to come out of St. Louis in twenty-five years. He won the 2010 NCAA Championship and earned his PGA Tour card in 2012.

My opening round got off to a fast start. I birdied the first and the third holes and added another birdie at the par-five sixth hole. I made a great save for a bogey on number eight and played the front nine in two under par. I made another birdie on number eleven, which felt like an eagle, because the par four plays a robust 498 yards. I birdied the sixteenth to put myself at four under for the day. The seventeenth hole is another beastly par four that measures 475 yards, and number eighteen plays 482 yards as a par four. I was able to scratch out par on those two monsters and post a four-under-par 66 to take the lead in the clubhouse. I struggled during the final two days of the tournament, posting scores of 73 and 74, but it was good enough to finish in sixth place and earn a $1,400 check. The first round of the event instilled a confidence in me that I would ride the rest of the summer. I continued my strong play in the Gateway Section, adding three more runner-up finishes that produced small checks of $450, $700, and $600.

One of the highlights of the summer was a Gateway Section Pro-Am at Algonquin Golf Club, where I was grouped with three members and my dad. One of the Algonquin members was a business client of my dad's, which is how we wound up paired together. I tore up the course and fired a five-under-par 66 to win the event by a shot and collect a nice little payday. It felt good to play so well in front of Dad and his client.

I was playing the best golf of my life and shooting low scores. My paychecks came in almost as frequently and consistently as I was taking my medicine.

* * *

By the end of August, I was starting to look toward Q-School, which would begin during the final week of October. My final event in the Section, in late September, cemented my belief that it was time to go back to Q-School. It was held at Old Warson Country Club, the site of the 1971 Ryder Cup. Old Warson is the most difficult golf course in the St. Louis metro area; it is heavily tree lined on every hole, with slick, undulated greens. I posted a two-under-par 69 for my fourth runner-up finish of the season, good for an $800 payday.

Par is a great score at Old Warson, and my score told me that I was ready for Q-School. However, I had one more event before heading to Dallas.

I was off to the Lake of the Ozarks, in central Missouri. I would partner with my old pal Rick Ewing. He was the long-time assistant pro at Old Warson. He was married with two young boys and a gorgeous wife; I was a stern bachelor. He has a technically sound golf swing, and I am a feel player with a swing that looks rather unconventional. We couldn't be more different, but we always partner well together.

The team event at the lake brings in the best club pros from St. Louis, Kansas City, and Tulsa. It is a bigger-money event, with somewhere in the neighborhood of $15,000 up for grabs in the most exciting of all gambling games, the Calcutta, which is when golfers bid on who will win a tournament and receive a percentage of the pot as winnings. Rick and I finished fifth out of twenty-five teams and both played well. Rick pitched in twice from off the green, and it seemed like I was making birdie on every other hole, making putts from everywhere. It was another solid paycheck for both of us, and I was playing well heading into Q-School.

* * *

Two days after the Lake Team Event, I made the ten-hour drive to Dallas from St. Louis. I arrived a week early so I could get familiar with the course, Stonebridge Ranch Country Club, which is just north of Dallas. Stonebridge is an Arthur Hills design, a 7,117-yard par seventy-two. I stayed on my good friend Chris Young's couch for the week prior to the actual tournament. Young and I played practice rounds for four days in a row, picking out my lines off the tees and getting a feel for the distances. I had recruited my brother to caddie for me, and he flew into Dallas two days before the start of the tournament. We ended up staying in a cottage on the golf course property for the week.

The first round was on my thirtieth birthday: October 30, 2007. There is nothing like the pressure on the first tee during the first round of Q-School. And so we began—me, Kevin, and my nerves.

The tenth hole at Stonebridge is a 390-yard uphill par four with out-of-bounds just left of the fairway. I nervously pulled my opening tee shot down the left side, but it stayed in bounds by a few yards. I smashed a pitching-wedge shot over the green and was able to get up and down to save a par.

My nerves were a major factor during the opening round. I had putted well all summer but now felt as if I was handcuffed on the greens, struggling to get my putts to the hole. I played my first nine holes in two over par. I hadn't shot over par in months, and those first nine holes were a shock to my system. I walked angrily to the tenth hole of the day and hit a wild tee shot to the right to make another bogey, which sent me into a tailspin for the rest of the round; I limped in with a five-over-par 77.

So much for the birthday mojo.

In order to advance to the second stage, I would have to finish in the top 19 players out of the 107 that were competing at Stonebridge. After the first round, I was tied for eightieth place.

The second round started off solid. I opened with eight pars in a row and birdied the ninth hole to move to one under for the day. But I was playing much better than that score. I was hitting greens and then hitting solid putts, but not many of those putts were disappearing into the hole. I needed to shoot an under par round to get back into the tournament. I missed from twelve feet for birdie on number ten, missed from fifteen feet for birdie at eleven, missed from twenty feet for birdie at twelve, missed again from eight feet for birdie at thirteen, and was getting hot under the collar. I saved par at fourteen and fifteen after missing both greens in regulation.

The sixteenth hole at Stonebridge is a 549-yard par five with out-of-bounds to the left and a lake running down the entire length of the right side of the fairway. It's a daunting tee shot, especially when the wind is freshening. I split the fairway with my tee ball and had 230 yards to the hole location. I played my nineteen-degree hybrid club to thirty feet above the hole and hit a solid eagle putt that took a peek into the hole on its way six feet past it, but my birdie putt would be easy and straight uphill. I got the feeling that I was going to make the putt and that this would get me to two under par for the day. But by thinking that way, my mind began looking into the future rather than staying in the present. I should have just continued focusing on one shot at a time. I missed that putt and set off a dangerous stream of anger inside of myself. As I walked off the sixteenth green, there had to have been smoke billowing from my ears.

When I got to the seventeenth tee, I wanted to choke myself. My blood was boiling. My anger had ruined things in my life away from golf, and now I was teetering on the border of allowing that same manic anger to wreck another round of golf.

The seventeenth hole at the Arthur Hills–designed Stonebridge Ranch Country Club is an uphill 328-yard par four. A nasty bunker lurks to the left of the fairway to gobble up any errant lay-up shots, and two more protect the front and left of the green. A water hazard runs down the entire right side of the hole and creeps in close to the right side of the green. There are two choices with this tee shot: take the driver and hit it short, left of the green, and try to get up and down for birdie or hit a four iron to 100 yards and attack the hole location with a wedge.

I looked at Kevin and said, "Fuck it. Driver, please."

"Roast it." He agreed.

My goal with this tee shot was to get my ball somewhere on the left side of the green or just left of the green to give me a good angle to pitch or chip to the back right hole location to set up a birdie. So I aimed at the left-hand green-side bunker and played my go-to fade shot, moving my ball left to right. The hole was playing downwind, so I knew I could get my drive all the way to the green. I am normally a 285- to 290-yard driver, but when you factor in the helping breeze, adrenaline, and anger, I was able to get a little extra.

I let it fly.

When my driver connected with the ball, I felt no contact whatsoever, no vibration of the shaft of my driver, nothing. My follow-through was something that Seve Ballesteros would have been proud of: I fell backward after hitting the ball and shuffled my feet to rebalance myself before walking toward my brother to give him the driver back. I saw that my ball had started at my target and was cutting back toward the green, so I quit watching the ball because I knew it would be in decent shape. My instinct told me the shot was solid.

As I handed my driver back to Kevin, I began taking off my glove, and I heard my playing partner, Jay McCluen, say, "That just went in."

"What?" I asked.

There was a spectator on the tee with us, a man who could have passed for Wilford Brimley. He said in his southern drawl, "Son, I think that ball went in the hole. I think I just saw that."

"I think so, too." My brother said as he put the head cover back on my driver.

"Come on, no way." I responded. "It had to have gone over the green, and you saw it disappear; it's downhill over this green."

Kevin and I walked a bit more briskly on this hole. Both of my playing partners had hit their tee shots into the front bunker. While they sized up their next shots, my brother and I approached the cup. My Titleist Pro V1X was in the bottom of the jar. It was a hole in one and an albatross—three strokes under par and the only bird in golf more rare than the eagle. It was very surreal.

I grabbed the ball and tossed it to my smiling brother. The shot immediately put me at four under par for the day. I was right back in it, but we still had one hole to play.

On the walk to the eighteenth tee box, my memory reverted back to something Jack Nicklaus said during his run to win the 1986 Masters, when his emotions were flowing:

"I kept reminding myself that I still had golf to play," Nicklaus said.

Nicklaus's humble words were ringing in my ears as we arrived on the eighteenth tee. I wanted to play the final hole of the day smart and not give back any of the shots that I had just gained.

The eighteenth hole at Stonebridge Ranch is a 457-yard par four. I blasted another driver down the right-hand side that crept into the rough. I had 120 yards left to the hole and played a wedge to twenty-five feet right of the hole and two-putted for par to card a 68. After signing my scorecard, Kevin and I enjoyed the feeling of being right in the middle of the tournament. We walked back to the car, quoting *Caddyshack* the entire time.

"Gambling is illegal at Bushwood, sir! And I never slice."

The finish to that round shot a jolt of confidence through me. I had gone from a month-long stay in a psychiatric ward and facing my parents in court to making a hole in one on a par four at the PGA Tour Q-School sixteen months later.

There had only been one other ace on a par four in a PGA Tour–sanctioned event before that. Andrew Magee had aced the seventeenth hole at TPC Scottsdale when his tee shot crashed into the putter of a player in the group in front of him, rolled toward the hole, and vanished for an amazing albatross. I realized that no matter what happened during the rest of the tournament, no one would ever be able to take that hole in one away from me.

The driver that I used for that shot was the exact same one I had been carrying with me during the manic episode when I took the baseball bat to my Honda on the side of the freeway in Southern Illinois. Even in my manic haze, I must have had a sixth sense that that club had some sort of importance in my golf future.

The third round of the 2007 Q-School was easy. It was a six-birdie, two-bogey round that produced another 68 and put me in good shape heading into the final day of the tournament. When I woke up on the morning of the final round, my lower back was frozen. I crumbled to my knees as soon as I got out of bed. I had never felt physical pain like this; I couldn't stand up straight. My brother noticed that I was writhing in pain and instructed me to lie down on the floor of the hotel room. He stretched my hamstrings by lifting my legs straight up in the air and pushing them toward my head, one leg at a time.

Here I was, three hours way from the most important round of my life with my legs up in the air, ready for traction rather than a tournament. The pressure of the moment, the constant wear and tear from my golf swing and sleeping on friends' couches had combined to freeze my body from waist to neck. But there was no way I would miss this round.

I went to the practice tee early and hit balls while Kevin continued the hamstring stretch after every fifth ball. It was loosening up enough to play, but it certainly felt odd. There is an old adage in tournament golf: "Always watch out for the injured golfer." My nerves were back, but I felt good, somehow. I think the adrenaline helped with my back spasms.

I played the front nine in one over par for a 37. I hit the ball well but didn't make many putts. I made solid pars at ten and eleven while my brother continued stretching my hamstrings at the tee boxes and in the fairways between almost every shot.

The twelfth hole was a major turning point. I had missed the green with my approach shot and was in the rough. As I stood over my third shot on that par four, my sand wedge grazed the ball, and it moved forward about a half an inch. I stopped and looked at my brother.

"Did you see that?" I asked him.

"What?" He answered.

"My wedge hit the ball forward."

"I didn't see it." He replied.

"Well, I did."

I had addressed the ball; therefore, it counted as a stroke. None of my playing partners had seen it, either. I wanted so badly to play well but I would never be able to live with myself if I didn't count that shot. I played my fourth shot on the green to about ten feet and missed the bogey putt. My playing partner, Scott Jamison, looked at me when I holed out and asked whether that was a bogey five on the hole.

"No sir. That was a double-bogey six." Now I was really behind the eight ball with not very many holes remaining.

I was three over for the day with only six holes left to play. The thirteenth hole at Stonebridge is a reachable par five, but I pulled my tee shot left of the fairway, and my ball came to rest on the cart path. If I were to have taken relief from the cart path and dropped my ball (with no penalty) at the nearest point of relief, my path for the shot would have been blocked out by overhanging trees so I elected to play the shot off the white cement cart path. I grabbed my nineteen-degree hybrid club and had to play a thirty-yard slice over the trees back toward the fairway. It was a gutsy play under any circumstances. That shot was my gambling instinct coming out. If I mishit that shot, the tournament was over for me. I picked the ball clean off the path, and my ball rose up quickly over the trees and cut back into play about forty yards short of the green in the fairway. The wedge distance was awkward, but I was able to get the ball to stop ten feet from the hole for a probable birdie. I rolled the putt into the center and grabbed the momentum back that I had lost on the previous hole. I made a solid par on number fourteen and then faced the daunting 190-yard par-three fifteenth hole. I blocked my tee shot with a six iron to the right of the putting surface and played a pitch to about fifteen feet above the hole.

The only thing I told myself before that putt was *Keep your fucking head still*. I never even looked up after I hit the putt; I waited until I heard my brother say, "Great save!" The ball had found the bottom of the cup.

The sixteenth hole was a par five that was reachable with a solid tee shot. I split that fairway and had 221 yards to the hole. I played another quality nineteen-degree hybrid to the center of the green, forty feet from the hole, and my eagle putt came up six feet short. My hands were trembling as I took the putter back for the birdie putt. The ball dove into the middle of the hole for another birdie.

Now it was on to my signature hole, the short par-four seventeenth. I hit another driver to the front edge of the green, pitched my second shot to two feet, and carded a clutch birdie. I had one-putted the last four greens in a row; my putter was hot. I smashed my tee shot on number eighteen down the right side of the fairway and had 125 yards to the hole. I played a wedge to twenty feet above the hole. I didn't read the putt for very long; I knew I was going to make it. The slick downhill putt broke sharply from my right to left and poured into the hole like water going down a drain for my third birdie in a row and a final-round score of 71.

My playing partners congratulated me on my strong finish, and we all shook hands. Now it was time to check the scoreboard after we signed our cards. I was inside the number by two shots and would move on to the second stage of Q-School for the first time in my career. I took a moment to myself after signing my scorecard, looked out over the golf course, and embraced what I had just accomplished. I had been working toward this type of performance since I was fourteen years old; I always knew I had it in me and I had finally proven it. I was ecstatic and exhausted.

I finally had a leg to stand on as a professional golfer, after all the years of struggling and fighting for my game. I was medicated, playing well, and healthy. The golf gods were guiding me.

THE FOURTEEN CLUBS

I stayed healthy throughout this period because of my rigorous schedule of exercise and medication and because I stayed busy, but my heavy drinking would soon cancel those effects.

7

THE CHASE TO IMPROVE

*Yes, sometimes I fail, but at least
I am willing to experiment.*
—*Bono*

I HAD FINALLY advanced to the second stage of Q-School. Playing the final six holes of the first-round tournament in four under par, including three birdies in a row to finish the final round, gave me a new high. But it was relief more than anything else. There was no secret to my success. It was old-fashioned, down in the trenches hard work. The thousands of hours of practice were finally paying off.

The high wasn't nearly as intense as a manic high, but it filled me with confidence that I had never felt before. I felt reborn as a golfer. It was similar to the feeling I had in 2001, when I won the St. Louis District Amateur, but better: I wasn't an amateur anymore. I was becoming a real professional.

I had ten days to prepare before the second stage, but I didn't know where I would play. I could be sent anywhere in the United States: California, Georgia, Florida, and North Carolina were all possibilities. There was also a chance I'd be sent back to Dallas for the second stage. In the meantime, I needed a place to practice for a week, to stay sharp. It was too cold at the beginning of November to play in St. Louis, so I called my old college teammate, Walter Anderson, who is a member of the Baton Rouge Country Club in Baton Rouge, Louisiana. He was happy to put me up for a few days while I waited on my second-stage assignment, so I made the drive from Dallas to Baton Rouge. By practicing on the very narrow BRCC golf course, with its very small fairways, I would improve my driving accuracy. I could test my short game, as well, on the slick and undulating greens.

Anderson had been the number-one player on our college golf team every year that we played together and had beaten Bubba Watson face-to-face in a college tournament. He had gone on to compete in the US Amateur in 1998. Naturally, I figured he would help keep me on my game. We worked on bunker shots and shaping iron shots in different directions and played plenty of different putting games on the practice green.

* * *

After four days practicing with Anderson in Baton Rouge, I finally got my assignment: TPC Craig Ranch in Dallas. On my way back to Dallas, my lower back began acting up again, most likely because I had been sleeping on floors and couches for a month and spending hours upon hours driving all over the country. My body was beginning to melt down. It literally took me twenty minutes to get out of my car to pump gas when I stopped in Shreveport. It felt as if someone was plunging a knife into the right side of my lower back, just above my beltline; my back was locked, and I couldn't stand up straight.

The four-hour drive from Shreveport to Dallas was excruciating. I had to lean my chin directly over the steering wheel to get relief from the burning and stinging radiating in my lower right side. Getting in and out of my car caused the worst pain that I had ever felt. This was the first serious physical issue I'd had in my entire athletic life to that point.

My good buddy Chris Young, with whom I was staying in Dallas, took one look at me and knew my body wasn't right. Chris, also known as "Coupon" because he was so tight with a dollar back in college, drove me all over Dallas in search of a cure to my lower-back pain. Our first stop was one of his client's chiropractic practice. It took ten minutes just to get me out of the car in the parking lot. I tried stretches, vibrating recliners, and yoga poses. None of it worked, so we looked elsewhere. I made frantic phone calls. Massage therapists didn't work, advice from an orthopedic surgeon was no good, and four hours with a physical therapist did nothing. I was hesitant to take painkillers, fearing they would interfere with the lithium.

I was two days away from the biggest golf tournament of my life, and I couldn't walk. I had always questioned athletes who cried "bad back"; I thought they were weak or faking it. That opinion changed in a hurry. I couldn't do simple everyday activities, let alone play golf. I was scared and my anger was growing. I felt like all the guys I would be playing against were practicing their asses off, and I was losing ground before the tournament even began.

Coupon was on my bag for the week, so we changed tack and went to TPC Craig Ranch to play a practice round. I popped ibuprofen like it was M&M's all day long, but it didn't help. I hobbled around the golf course like an old man.

I painfully chopped my way through the first practice round only two days before the event started. I tried to play the final practice round, but I couldn't. I could only get my driver shots to about 230 yards, much less than my usual 290. Yardage like that would spell D-O-O-M for me on a course like TPC Craig Ranch, where it is always windy and length off the tee is essential to score well. As Coupon and I approached the eleventh tee during the last practice day, I couldn't take it anymore.

"Coupon, let's go." I said as I began heading for the parking lot.

"Where are we going?" he asked.

"To get a shot in my back; there is no way I can compete like this. We have to find one of those urgent care places." I realized how pro baseball players and football players must feel when trying to play through injury.

We found an urgent care center just a few miles from the golf course. I told the doctor my predicament, and he suggested a low-dose cortisone shot that would give me five to seven days or relief.

Within two hours of the shot, I felt no pain. I went back to the golf course to pound golf balls until dark to prepare for the tournament. It was a miraculous turnaround. I went from not being able to walk to ripping my driver as far as I have ever hit it.

* * *

Four good rounds separated me from the final stage of Q-School and a chance for status on either the PGA Tour or the Web.com Tour.

The second stage of Q-School was filled with great players like Colt Knost, Notah Begay, Peter Tomasulo, Tag Ridings, Erik Compton, and

Michael Block. I had watched some of these guys in major championships on television and was now competing against them. The golf ball reps were in the lobby of the clubhouse, giving away balls and gloves. It was surreal, but Coupon kept me grounded.

Still, I didn't score well; my tempo was off the entire week, and I posted rounds of 79–72–74–76 to miss moving on to the final stage by a mile. But I played pain free, so I couldn't blame any of my poor showing on my back. I think some of the natural adrenaline from the week added to the cortisone worked overtime to maintain my crumbling body. The truth is that I had given everything I had to get through the first stage. My body and my mind were fried by the time I got to the second stage.

During my third round, we were paired with Steven Bowditch, who was on his way back up to the PGA Tour after two years of public battles with his own depression. I didn't bring up my disorder with him on the golf course during our round together, but I wish I had. I was still stuck in my own bipolar closet. He was a fun guy to play with and ultratalented. I had worn my patent leather red, white, and blue saddle shoes during our round together, and he liked them.

"Nice wheels, mate," he told me on the first tee in his down-under accent.

Bowditch didn't score very well while we were paired, but he did fire a course-record 64 the next day to show that he was on the rise. He went on to win the PGA Tour in 2014. I always root for him when I see his name on a leaderboard.

* * *

As soon as the tournament was over, I had to drive from Dallas to Hilton Head, South Carolina, where my family had gathered to celebrate Thanksgiving and my parents' thirty-fifth wedding anniversary. With another long drive and the cortisone shot wearing off, I was in real trouble and the drive turned ugly midway through. I had to lean over the steering wheel again to relieve pressure and pain in my lower back. Any other position resulted in sharp, brutal pain.

By the time I arrived in Hilton Head, I couldn't stand up straight. My parents were so concerned that they took me to the emergency room.

Not another fuckin' hospital!

We joked about being at the hospital for my back instead of for my bipolar disorder while we waited for the test results, which revealed a herniated disc and a pinched sciatic nerve. Both are injuries that golfers deal with often. I'd be out of commission for the last two months of 2007; my body needed the rest.

I was physically out of gas, but my mental health was strong. I was taking my medicine every morning and just needed some rest in order to get my body back in order. Then I could get back to traveling and playing tournaments. I planned to be back on the horse by the end of the year.

* * *

2008 proved to be a very average year on the golf course for me. I continued to compete in the Gateway PGA Section events and winning small paychecks, but I didn't achieve any noticeable success or make dramatic improvement to my game. I think getting so close to the final stage at Q-School and not advancing knocked my confidence down a little.

On the bipolar front, I kept my illness in check. I hadn't had any sign of mania or depression since the pivotal summer of 2006 and thought I had put it all behind me. The hearing and the twenty-six-day hospital stay were burned into my memory, and I was committed to taking my lithium daily to stay healthy.

I focused on teaching lessons and working on my own golf game, and I decided not to go to the 2008 Q-School in the fall. I felt like I needed to improve my short game in order to get to the next level, so I took a job at Andalusia at Coral Mountain, in La Quinta, California.

I fell in love with Andalusia, especially the short-game practice area behind the driving range, when I visited in February 2008. It's short-game heaven: three huge, sloping greens with great bunkers. I could work in peace and quiet at the base of Palm Desert's gorgeous Santa Rosa Mountains. I took the job at Andalusia specifically to use its practice area.

The job humbled me. I worked outside service, which means I handled valet duty when members of the club arrived, cleaned and staged golf carts, set up and picked the driving range, and caddied. It was not glamorous work, but I loved it. The people I worked with were great, and I made friends with most of the Andalusia staff. I earned a steady paycheck, I was allowed to work on my golf game, and I networked for possible sponsorships that would allow me to return to the road to play tournaments after the job at Andalusia ended. I was healthy, living a "normal" life, taking my medicine every morning, and in great shape because the job kept me moving. I drank from time to time, but never excessively when I lived in La Quinta. Although there were mornings when I woke up with a hangover, they were few and far between.

By the end of my time at Andalusia, my golf game was razor sharp and I looked forward to going out on the road and testing myself. I left Southern California at the end of April 2009 and headed back to St. Louis for the US Open Local Qualifying at Persimmon Woods Golf Club. I shot a disappointing 77, and missed qualifying by five strokes. But I didn't have time to pout. I left St. Louis just a few days later to compete in my first NGA Hooters Tour Event at Quail Crossing Golf Course in Boonville, Indiana.

* * *

The NGA Hooters Tour is the longest-running mini tour in the United States. The events are run very well, and the circuit is a great place for players to experience the lifestyle of a professional golfer. Many great players have started out on this developmental tour and continued on to make a living playing professional golf. Alums like Keegan Bradley, Lee Janzen, Zach Johnson, David Toms, Jim Furyk, and Tom Lehman have even won major championships after playing on the NGA Tour. British Open champion Ben Curtis and Masters champion Bubba Watson both played the tour.

I had never played an NGA Tour event, and I was nervous. Fortunately it proved to be a positive turning point in my career. I shot 68–69–68–70 to finish somewhere near thirtieth place. Thirtieth place may not seem like a very good finish, but I looked at it as a major positive. To make the cut and earn a paycheck on a proven professional golf tour in my first attempt gave me a boost in confidence.

I drove away from Boonville feeling good—my game was improving. If the bipolar mind can accept and embrace the commitment to constantly improve, the disorder can be managed with ease.

* * *

I got a phone call from my old buddy Walter Anderson, who worked for Merrill Lynch at the time. His company was sponsoring an event on the Adams Tour, another of the developmental tours that runs through the South. Walter said he could get me into the tournament that was held at the University Club in Baton Rouge. I jumped at the opportunity and a week after the NGA Hooters event, I headed to Walter's.

It was scorching in the bayou. The temperatures were around 105 degrees, and the humidity in Baton Rouge was suffocating. I always play well when it's really hot, so I wasn't concerned.

I opened with a solid round of 70 while carrying my own bag. Afterward, I felt like I had gone twelve rounds with Muhammad Ali; I was beat. Fortunately, I'd have Walter on the bag for my second round. He is a perfect caddie and also a great player in his own right. I trust him.

I played the front nine in one under par but needed to pick up the pace if I was going to make the cut to play the weekend. I hit the ball to eight feet for birdie on the tenth hole but missed. I hit it to twelve feet for birdie on eleven and missed. I hit it to fifteen feet for birdie on number twelve and missed again. I hit it inside of ten feet on holes thirteen and fourteen but missed those birdie putts as well. At the fifteenth tee box, the Adams Tour had set up a scoreboard showing what the projected cut was looking like. I was three under for the tournament, but the projected cut was currently at five under. I needed to birdie two of the last four holes to make the cut. This was the first time in a tournament when I knew what I had to do going down the stretch.

After I hit my tee shot on number fifteen, Walter told me I was being too tentative with my birdie putts. "You need to putt to *make* those putts. It looks like you are putting just to get the ball close, instead of being aggressive and trying to get them into the cup," he coached me.

He was right. I was apprehensive because I didn't want to get sloppy and three-putt. I needed to be aggressive and let the putts go more freely. With this in mind, I hit a miraculous bounce-up wedge into the fifteenth green from a horrible lie in the left rough to fifteen feet for another good look at a birdie. I told myself that I wouldn't move my head on the putt and I would stroke the putt solidly.

"Great putt, good birdie." Walter encouraged me after my ball found the hole. One birdie down, one more to make the cut with three holes to play.

I ripped a five iron to the back of the green and left myself a twisting, turning birdie putt from about forty feet on the sixteenth hole, a 210-yard par three. I hit a great putt that took a look into the hole before racing six feet past the cup. The six-footer for par was a must-make. I pretended my head was in cement and knocked it in for par.

On the seventeenth hole, a 570-yard dogleg-left par five, I hit a quality drive and left myself 265 yards to the hole from the middle of the fairway. I chose my three wood and played a low bullet of a shot that was pushed to the right side of the green by a breeze. My ball came to rest about thirty-five feet from the hole, giving me a chance for the eagle. I put a great roll on a putt that finished stone dead just a foot away from the hole. I tapped in for birdie and made it to five under for the tournament.

The final hole at the U Club that day was a 435-yard par four. I played my customary low fade to the center of the fairway, which left me 147 yards to the back right hole location. I played a smooth nine-iron shot that hunted the flag the entire time it was in the air. My ball landed five feet to the right of the cup, spun directly left, and stopped just two inches shy of the hole. Another tap-in birdie to close my day, getting me to six under par for the first thirty-six holes of the event. I made the cut with one shot to spare.

The finish to that round is almost identical to the finish during the final round at Stonebridge Ranch, where I birdied the final three holes to advance in the Q-School. This time, I knew what I needed to accomplish on the final four holes, and I did just that—plus a bonus birdie. To be able to play my best golf with my back against the wall, for the second time, told me I was growing as a player.

I left the scorching heat of Louisiana and traveled back to the same scorching heat in St. Louis. The summer of 2009 was off to a good start for me: I had played in two events on two different professional tours and made the cut for both. The thrilling finish to the second round in Baton Rouge was something I will always remember. When I returned home, I had two weeks off before I would fly to the West Coast to compete in the Long Beach Open.

* * *

An assistant pro at my favorite course in St. Louis, Fox Run Golf Club, left me a voice mail message about a caddying job. Fox Run was hosting the US Junior Amateur Qualifier, and a man from New York had called the pro shop at Fox Run in search of a caddie for his thirteen-year-old son. I was happy to take the job. I didn't know whether this kid could even break 90, but I needed the money because I hadn't yet secured a sponsor for my own golf career. The kid—whoever he was—would have his hands full in the qualifier, thirty-six holes in one day on a course ranked as the most difficult golf course in the state of Missouri.

When I arrived on the driving range on the morning of the qualifier, I noticed a young kid absolutely striping iron shot after iron shot as his dad watched from behind him. The sound the ball made coming off the kid's clubs was the same sound you hear at a PGA Tour event. As I watched in awe, the father approached me.

"Mike?"

"Yes, sir."

"I am Mike Liu. Are you here to caddie for my son Jim?" he said in English with a thick Chinese accent.

"Yes, Mr. Liu. I am your man today. I know the course very well, and think I can help out your boy. Is this him?" I began to get excited when I realized that I would be caddying for the kid who had caught my eye when I stepped on the practice range.

"Yes. Jim, come over here. This is Mr. Wellington."

"Please, Jimmy, you can call me Mike."

"Nice to meet you, Mike. Thank you for caddying for me today."

The kid may have only been thirteen, but he demonstrated the maturity of a thirty-five-year-old man. He had my attention right from the start of our first round together. He didn't hit a cut shot or a draw shot; he hit every shot dead straight. It was pure joy to watch Jimmy Liu play.

He made his way around the toughest course in the state of Missouri with ease. He posted rounds of 72 and 73, playing from 7,100 yards. I knew I was watching something special; he was a prodigy. He hit lots of greens in regulation and had a syrupy putting stroke, and he got better and better as the day progressed. He qualified with ease that day and went on to make the match-play portion of the US Junior Amateur later in the summer. I learned that young Jimmy Liu had shot 59 when he was nine years old at another junior tournament. This was quite the introduction to a player I would see again, without a doubt.

* * *

After caddying for Jimmy, I headed west to compete in the Long Beach Open. My friend Blake Moore from Pasadena, who had told me about the tournament, let me stay at his apartment for the event. Blake is a powerful player and cutthroat competitor from Southern California who played at the University of Colorado.

I played decently at Long Beach, shooting two under par for the first thirty-six holes of the tournament. I needed to shoot four under to make the cut. Missing the cut sent me into some dangerous territory; I spent the rest of that weekend drinking—big mistake.

It is now my belief that someone with bipolar disorder should never consume alcohol. Alcohol is a natural depressant, which is the last thing anyone who suffers from manic depression needs. My ego was taking control of me again, except this time it wasn't spinning me into mania; it was leading me down the hallway of depression right into a room of despair.

I was taking my lithium every day, but keeping bipolar disorder in check is more than just taking medication. You must remain healthy in every aspect of your life: eating right, exercising, sticking to a routine, and not drinking. There are no shortcuts to managing bipolar disorder, and just when you think you have it under control . . . it jumps up and bites you.

After missing the cut at the Long Beach Open, I traveled to Houston and missed another cut on the NGA Tour. I left Houston and headed to

Philadelphia, Mississippi, for another NGA Tour event. My confidence was ebbing.

The event in Mississippi was held at a large resort called the Dancing Rabbit. The resort features a casino and a beautiful golf course carved out of the trees, with creeks and lakes running throughout the property. It is nature at its finest. But even on a beautiful piece of land like that, my depression was blinding my view of anything else.

I went out for a practice round by myself before the tournament started. I always enjoy playing by myself and getting to know a golf course before a tournament, but this round was unlike any I had ever played. I found myself walking down the fairways in tears. I was living my dream, traveling city to city, playing professional golf tournaments. How could I possibly be depressed with my dream unfolding around me? Finally, I realized that it was my illness. It was the first time I realized that depression is a very real thing. I had had bouts of depression before, but those were all following manic episodes. This depression came out of nowhere and was attacking me; there was nothing I could do to stop it. On a beautiful bright summer day, I had to walk off the ninth hole during a practice round because I couldn't control the tears that were streaming down my face.

I got myself together enough to play the first round of the tournament, but as I warmed up before the round, I didn't have any nerves. I didn't feel nervous when I got to the first tee, either; I felt no emotions at all. Usually, my adrenaline is pumping and my nerves are jangling on the first tee of a tournament. I love that feeling, but it was absent on this day.

I shot 78 numbed with depression. I felt like I was disrespecting the game by trying to play with a black cloud over me. I withdrew from the tournament and drove back to St. Louis. I had never withdrawn from a tournament before, and I was not proud of it. I had been taught to always finish a golf tournament that I had started, even if it meant posting a score of 100. I made it through the first round, but I couldn't go back out on course, slopping my golf ball around with no energy.

As I drove home, I decided that I would skip Q-School 2009 and step away from the game. My mind wasn't where it needed to be. It had been flipped around in just forty-five days from healthy flow to booze-induced lethargy.

I wanted to get as far away from that anxiety as I could, so I began self-medicating. When I felt down I'd drink a few 7 and 7s to numb myself. I stayed out late every night and slept late every morning. Whiskey and beer were tearing me down. I felt stupid and slow: I lost my quick wit. But I continued to take my lithium, so I thought I would be fine. It is so easy to see the error in your ways in retrospect but inside the haze of depression and drug abuse, nothing is clear or easy.

It is possible that I had been setting myself up for a bout of depression by continuing to play tournaments without a sponsor. Support was very important for me . . . professionally, financially, and personally; it is what enabled me, and still does, to be the best I can be. Every missed cut brought me greater anxiety about my lack of sponsorships and opened a new pipeline to depression.

Back to St. Louis, I needed income. My time on the road had drained my already depleted bank account, so I returned to teaching golf lessons and caddying.

But I could not give up my dream. I just couldn't.

In a drunken haze on the night before the 2009 Q-School application was due, I wrote an email of desperation to a friend, asking for the $4,500 entry fee. I wouldn't be able to live with myself if I gave up on Q-School after spending the last year preparing to compete. My friend agreed to cover the $4,500 for me, no strings attached.

I filed my entry the next day and waited for my assignment. Ironically, I was sent back to Stonebridge Ranch, where the magic had happened for me two years earlier. But there was no magic this time around; it was a disaster. I was so depressed that I didn't even hire a caddie for the tournament. I thought I could do it all by myself again. It was ridiculous not to have a caddie at a tournament event. The disorder owned my decision-making.

I shot rounds of 77, 81, 76, and 71. I was a mess, and when I drove back to St. Louis, I really felt that my career playing professional golf was over. Kaput. I really needed to take that break from the game to get out from under the depression.

I needed to find a job, so that's exactly what I did.

* * *

When I returned to St. Louis in late October, after a disastrous showing at Q-School, I learned about an opportunity in broadcasting. My experience as a color commentator with the Missouri Tigers helped get me an audition for a job with InsideSTL.com.

Tim McKernan, a well-known St. Louis radio host with a very successful morning show in St. Louis sports talk radio, wanted to create a new show in partnership with his emerging website, InsideSTL.com. I landed the job after a series of auditions, one of which included sitting in on McKernan's morning show. I would cohost *Nick and the Badger* with McKernan's producer–sidekick, Joe Pelusi and Fox 2 sports reporter Charlie Marlow. There was no real meaning behind the show's name, which was a practice regularly embraced by all of McKernan's programming. The people of St. Louis ate it up.

THE FOURTEEN CLUBS

Drinking can be dangerous when it is combined with bipolar disorder. Alcohol is a natural depressant, and overindulging violates several of the Fourteen Clubs, even if you are otherwise successful at following them. Drinking is self-medication, so it interferes with your actual medication; it is not part of a healthy diet; it can make exercise difficult; and it usually destroys a solid routine. This time, for me, it caused a serious depressive episode, and it was only going to get worse.

8

RADIO, DRUGS, AND BOOZE

I can accept failure, but I can't accept not trying.
—*Michael Jordan*

"WE ARE BACK with me, 'Producer' Joe Pelusi; Michael 'Beef' Wellington; and Charlie 'Chuckles' Marlow on InsideSTL.com. This is *Nick and the Badger*."

On January 4, 2010, I made my debut as cohost of Tim McKernan and Joe Pelusi's brainchild, *Nick and the Badger*. Pelusi played the role of point man for the show, bringing us in and out of commercial breaks and introducing new topics for us to discuss. Marlow, a FOX-2 sports reporter, was the most naturally talented of our threesome. I was the smart-ass, slipping in a one-liner here and there for a few laughs. It was a blast.

The show had no real focus but had a sports flavor. We covered everything from timely sports stories to dating, celebrity disgraces, and anything in between. There was a lot of gambling talk, too. This was a format that was embraced by McKernan's morning show, and we followed his format as an extension of that program.

The job kept me busy. I had to do constant research within the sports world in order to be sharp when I was on the air. I watched Tony Kornheiser and Michael Wilbon on ESPN's *Pardon the Interruption* religiously. I read the entire sports sections of newspapers from all over the country, paying special attention to statistics. I listened to local and national radio shows to learn what was interesting to a radio listener and what to avoid as a host. I became a student of the sports broadcasting business.

My only experience in broadcasting to that point had been strictly in play-by-play, which I still feel is a much easier format than talk radio. In play-by-play, everything happens for you; all you have to do is describe and explain what you see. Talk radio is a completely different animal. You must be constantly on your toes.

Our show was second from the bottom in the ratings during our time slot, only ahead of a show that had achieved a zero rating. McKernan pulled the plug on the experimental show after six months. Our ratings weren't very good, and McKernan was switching radio stations, so it was time to kill the *Badger*.

Working on *Nick and the Badger* did so many things for me, positive and not-so-positive. I met wonderful people who worked for McKernan at his InsideSTL.com office. The job got my mind away from golf; I didn't touch a golf club for a solid three months, and by the middle of March my love of the game returned. On a less than positive note, the job reinforced for me that bipolar disorder has an enormous stigma attached to it. Many callers and guests on our show made uneducated references to bipolar disorder. The comments were backhanded slurs at anyone who was perceived to be acting strangely. I heard the phrase "He is probably bipolar" too many times to count but I never opened my mouth. In retrospect, I should have. But I remained silent to avoid outing myself to my cohosts.

By the time the first week of June rolled around, it was time to get back to golf; I missed it. I think many tournament golfers experience ups and downs in their love of the game. In many ways, the highs and lows of a tournament golfer mirror that of bipolar disorder: The highs are orgasmic, and the lows are difficult to handle. The *Badger* job pulled me out of a depression, so I am grateful for that time on the air.

* * *

In the summer of 2010, I hosted the seventeenth annual Firecracker 500, my own charity golf tournament held during the week of the Fourth of July. The tournament began in 1993 with two foursomes; by 2010, the tournament committee had grown the event to seventy-two players. Proceeds haven been donated to organizations such as the American Diabetes Association, Patriot Golf Day, the Alzheimer's Association of St. Louis, and the St. Louis Children's Hospital. For the 2010 event, I wanted to

donate the proceeds to promoting depression and bipolar disorder awareness. Because I thought I was in remission, had beaten the disease, I felt it
was important to raise money to help those who were still struggling with
the trials and tribulations of the illness. Little did I know, I hadn't escaped
the disorder at all.

I had great support in running the event from the National Alliance
for Mental Illness and former NFL Pro-Bowl punter Greg Montgomery,
who has been fighting against bipolar disorder for the better part of twenty
years. We met on the driving range at TPC Scottsdale where we immediately became friendly discussing our experiences with the disorder. The
2010 Firecracker Tournament raised $4,000 for the Depression Bipolar
Support Alliance. It felt great to give back.

My 2010 could not have been going better. I was getting ready to go
back on the road to compete in tournaments in preparation for the 2010
Q-School, and I hadn't seen any manic signals or behavior since the summer of 2006. I had kept the mania in check for four years and felt as if I
had buried it forever.

* * *

Before I could begin my own tournament season in 2010, Jimmy Liu
returned to St. Louis for the US Junior Amateur qualifier and asked me to
be on his bag for another marathon thirty-six-hole day. The course was a
stern, 7,200-yard test at Aberdeen Golf Club, a public facility about twenty-five miles southwest of St. Louis.

"Of course I will be there, little bro. See you at Aberdeen." I jumped at
the chance to watch Jimmy play golf.

The young master put on one of the greatest ball-striking displays that I
have ever seen. Jimmy Liu went around Aberdeen in 68–68, won the qualifier by four shots, and didn't bogey once. He could loft 225-yard shots that
landed like wedges next to the hole all day long. It was pure joy to watch
him play. The best part was that there was no ego involved: He wasn't
arrogant. He was a gentleman. He was also patient, kind to his playing
partners, and he played with amazing poise.

We shared a hug after he won the qualifier; he was on his way to his second US Junior Amateur at the ripe old age of fourteen. I was off to the great state of Maine for the Bangor Open.

*　*　*

I arrived in Maine with a fresh new mind-set, but I wasn't sure how my golf game would be after such a long layoff. The Bangor Open was my first tournament of 2010. I made sure to pack my lithium in my luggage.

The first hole of the tournament assured me that I was in the right place, back in tournament golf. I found the fairway with my tee shot, leaving 127 yards left to the hole. I chose my fifty-two-degree gap wedge and took dead aim. The ball landed ten feet short of the hole, took one bounce toward the flagstick, grabbed the green with a touch of backspin, and spilled over the front edge of the cup for an eagle two. The golf gods were welcoming me back.

I posted 68 in my first round and felt excited to be back on the road chasing the dream. The tournament in Maine was the first of a five-tournament schedule from July through September to give me a strong preparation for the 2010 Q-School. My performance in the 2009 Q-School was dreadful and embarrassing, but I didn't let it haunt me. Instead, it propelled my return to the sport I love and drove my determination to succeed in Q-School. Nothing was going to get in my way this year.

I played solidly in the second round of the Bangor Open, posting a 70, to make the cut with ease. I got a phone call as I drove out of Maine. Young Jimmy Liu was making history at the US Junior Amateur over in Michigan. At fourteen years old he had broken Tiger Woods's record as the youngest player to ever win that tournament. His play was legendary: In the thirty-six hole championship match, Jimmy's opponent shot 67 in the morning round and was three down to Jimmy's 64. By winning the US Junior Amateur title, Jimmy had won automatic berth in the Men's US Amateur in Washington State, at Chambers Bay, at which Mike asked me to caddie for Jimmy. He also invited me to the Liu's place at Pinehurst, North Carolina, to help Jimmy prepare for the US Amateur. Since I was already on the East Coast, I could stop in Washington, DC, to visit Johnny Mullin, and then head south to Pinehurst. I'd practice with Jimmy before we departed for the US Amateur. The caddie job would pay well; I had saved about half the Q-School entry fee, and the week on Jimmy's bag would cover the other half. Plus, I loved being with the kid, and it was a Major USGA Championship.

Fuck the mini tours, I thought. *Let's go check out what golf is like at a major.* Any serious golfer will tell you that you would be an idiot to turn down an invitation to Pinehurst.

I had to rearrange my own tournament schedule in order to caddie, which was fine by me, and I would be able to use the time at Pinehurst to work on my own game while helping Jimmy prepare for Chambers Bay.

* * *

While I was visiting Mullin in DC, I began experimenting with Adderall—a drug that is prescribed to people diagnosed with attention-deficit disorder. Do I have ADD? No. This was obviously a bad decision.

Many of my friends have ADD, and they all told me that Adderall helped increase their ability to focus on what they needed to do: work, school, and so on. I felt like my practice sessions since being on the East Coast had been sluggish, so I decided to try it.

I got my hands on Adderall, which is an amphetamine, from an old college friend who lived in DC, and I began taking it before going to the course to practice. My practice sharpened immediately. I was more focused, and I could practice longer without getting tired. I was self-medicating again, in the hopes of improving my golf game. I was starting to play well again. In fact, I was starting to play so well that I began putting with my eyes closed. The freedom of closing my eyes led to putts sinking from everywhere. As long as my golf was good, I could rationalize any type of behavior—or drug choice, in this case.

My confidence as a golfer was overflowing into cockiness. My five days in DC initiated a dangerous pattern, and it stuck with me afterward. I started each day by taking an Adderall and my lithium for breakfast, then went to work on my short game for four hours. I'd drink a Bloody Mary before lunch, and take more Adderall after lunch before playing a round of golf. After the round, I would practice putting (with my eyes closed) and then meet Mullin at the bar and binge drink until closing time. The combination of my golf game taking good form, my new focus from the Adderall, putts going in from everywhere with my eyes closed, and the excitement of knowing that I would soon be in America's golf capital had me feeling invincible. In retrospect, I can see that I was hypomanic and heading toward full-blown mania.

* * *

The Liu's condo sits on a fairway at the No. 5 course of Pinehurst Resort. Pinehurst is a piece of American golf history; it has hosted the PGA Championship, the US Open, the US Amateur, and the Ryder Cup. There are nine great golf courses—each of them identified by a number—on the property at Pinehurst, some of which were designed by course architect icons such as Donald Ross, Rees Jones, and Tom Fazio. I would have two days to myself at the condo, right in the middle of golf heaven, before Jimmy and Mike arrived.

On the first day, I explored every inch of the Village of Pinehurst, learning the lay of the land. I figured out where each golf course was located and came across dozens of other courses that aren't on the resort's property. I topped off the day at the legendary Carolina Inn where I ordered a drink in the Ryder Cup Lounge. I walked around the room, inspecting photos of past US Ryder Cup teams and touching replica trophies as the condensation from my 7 and 7 cocktail dripped from the Collins glass.

After a day of exploring, I was ready to get to work. Thoughts and ideas ran through my brain at a breakneck pace. I started the day with 1,200 milligrams of lithium and a rigorous, manic workout; the intensity put me into a good mood, skyrocketing my mania to new levels. Then I picked a course where I could practice, hopped in my rental car, popped an Adderall, and drove to the selected course with the radio blaring Lady Gaga.

That music choice illustrates the state of mind I was in. A thirty-one-year-old man listening to Lady Gaga. Seriously? Someone should have pulled me out of my car and taken me to a hospital immediately.

Mania heightened the five senses and erased my awareness of the world around me; taking Adderall intensified that awareness, giving me a great—but in no way healthy—mind-set in which to play golf.

The only time I was really able to focus was on the golf course, which made my practice sessions miraculous. I practiced for at least eight and sometimes twelve hours per day, including my time with Jimmy. I would practice at one course for an hour or so and then hop in my car, bite an Adderall in half, swallow it, then head for the next course, drunk and speeding. Many times, I had to pull over because I was crying so hard. Crying jags are part of my disorder, but I thought I was shedding tears of pure joy—because I had turned a corner with my golf game; because I wasn't in a hospital; because I could play golf every day instead of sitting in a cubicle; because I was able to walk, was a free American in a safe country, wasn't dead—not tears of a manic episode.

Time on the golf course was magnificent. I played 255-yard shots to within a foot of the hole. I hit whatever shot I wanted off the tee—high fades, high draws, low and piercing straight shots. It felt like a magnet pulled my ball into the hole on every putt. And every putt sent adrenaline through my body, pushing my mania closer to eruption. My ballooning confidence had become cockiness and the old feeling of invincibility.

My seven days at Pinehurst were the freest I had ever felt on the golf course. I felt like I could beat anybody you put in front of me.

* * *

After six days of intense practice, Jimmy and I were going to play Pinehurst No. 4. As a friend, I wanted to play with him because we hadn't yet done so. As a big brother figure, I wanted to stroll the fairways together and talk shop. Jimmy had traveled the country over the course of the year, playing extremely competitive tournaments with some of the best amateur players in the world, some of them twenty years older than him.

As a competitor, I wanted to kick his ass.

Before we began the round, I told Jimmy that he should play a lot of long-iron shots, because he would have a lot of those at the upcoming US Amateur. He played the extra shots, but he played out his first ball on every hole. I have played with many great players, but this match felt like playing with Bubba Watson, Hank Kuehne, Jay Delsing, or Jim Holtgrieve. Great players simply elevate the play of other golfers in their group.

The match went back and forth all day. At the par-four first hole, I blocked my opening tee shot into a fairway bunker on the right side of the hole. Jimmy split the fairway and hit a wedge to within fifteen feet for a good look at birdie. I had 111 yards from the trap and played a pure gap wedge that almost went into the hole but stopped just a few inches away for a tap-in birdie. Jimmy missed, and I went one up.

Jimmy birdied the par-five second hole and the par-four third hole, to go one up on me. I made bogey at the par-three fourth hole, to fall two down. I was letting a fourteen-year-old kid beat up on me. I made birdie on the 450-yard par-four fifth hole to get a hole back.

We both made par on six, seven, and eight. So I was one down standing on the tee at the par-five ninth hole. I sliced my tee shot into the pine trees on the right and had 261 yards to the hole. My ball was sitting on moist pine straw, and I had low-hanging trees that wouldn't allow me to launch a three-wood shot very high. I would have to play a low, rising shot to get my ball to the green.

Jimmy was sitting perfectly in the fairway, just 235 yards from the hole. He would most likely knock his ball on the green to set up an eagle putt.

I visualized my long shot starting out low and then climbing into the sky before landing softly on the putting surface and the shot came off exactly how I had pictured it. It began low and hovered over the ground before passing under the low-hanging trees and immediately rising to a towering height. It was heading right at the flagstick, attacking it like a heat-seeking missile. The ball landed on the front of the green, rolled toward the hole, and stopped only two feet from the cup.

Jimmy played a four iron to the heart of the green and two-putted for an easy birdie, but my eagle won the hole.

All square after nine holes.

I used the momentum to win the tenth with par to go one stroke up. We both made par on the beastly 451-yard eleventh hole. Jimmy made birdie on me at the 210-yard par-three twelfth hole to square the match. I two-putted for birdie on the par-five thirteenth to grab the lead again.

The fourteenth hole at Pinehurst is a 229-yard par three with water guarding the entire left side of the green and bunkers short of the green. The pin was cut no more than eight steps from the water, and the flagstick was perched on the front left corner of the green. I bailed out and played my ball thirty feet right of the hole for safety. Jimmy then played a four iron that sounded like a gunshot. His ball hunted the flag the entire time it was in the air and landed like a butterfly with sore feet just a foot from the hole. His kick-in birdie won the hole and squared the match again.

I played a two iron and a nine iron on the 381-yard par-four fifteenth hole to three feet for another birdie of my own to take a one-up advantage over Jimmy's par. We halved the 405-yard, par-four sixteenth hole, and I stayed one up. Jimmy made a great birdie on the 548-yard, par-five seventeenth hole to square the match, and we headed to the final hole.

The eighteenth at Pinehurst No. 4 is a 456-yard, dogleg-left par four that has a sinister green with undulations all over the putting surface. We both split the fairway with our tee shots and both hit our approach shots over the green. I played first for the third shot with my sixty-degree wedge. I would have to hit a lob shot straight up in the air to land the ball softly, because I only had about fifteen feet of green to work with, and it was downhill to the hole location. I executed the shot well, and my ball ended up eight feet past the hole for an uphill look at par. But the young phenom played a beautiful lob shot of his own that finished only six feet from the cup, just inside my ball. I lined up my par-saving putt and missed it to the left of the hole. Jimmy drilled his six-footer in to win the match one up.

He had shot 67 to my 68 and beaten me fair and square. On one hand, my mania was riled by a loss to a kid who couldn't even drive yet, but on the other, Jimmy played like a champion and I had stayed with him the entire round.

* * *

The day after the Pinehurst match with Jimmy Liu, I flew back to St. Louis for a few days before leaving for the caddie job at the US Amateur at Chambers Bay. I was still deeply engulfed in mania, still using Adderall, and still drinking. Thankfully, nothing strange happened before leaving for Washington State.

I brought my golf clubs with me on the trip to Chambers Bay so that I could continue to work hard on my own game in preparation for Q-School in my free moments. I was sober the entire time. I ran out of Adderall, and I decided that I wasn't going to drink at all while I was caddying. My mania calmed down during this weeklong hiatus from drugs and alcohol—concrete proof that sobriety and proper medication slow down mania. I took my lithium every morning, but without the Adderall and booze in my system, my mind moved slower, and I was better able to concentrate on the task at hand, which was doing my best to get Jimmy past the thirty-six-hole qualifying round and into the top sixty-four players who reach the match-play portion of the US Amateur Championship.

Chambers Bay is an absolute beast of a golf course that sits just above Puget Sound. The course is an enormous wind tunnel, with gorgeous views on every hole. It is a links-style course that is severely penalizing to any errant shot. Jimmy ended up missing the match-play portion by three strokes, but for a fourteen-year-old kid, his score was a tremendous accomplishment. He will have plenty of cracks at the US Amateur in his future, and I was honored to carry his bag.

* * *

My sobriety didn't last. I immediately fell into my old habits of binge drinking and popping Adderall when I got back to St. Louis, and the mania spiked again. I was so excited about my golf game being sharp that nothing mattered except getting high, getting drunk, and playing golf. I had three weeks to prepare for Q-School, held in San Antonio that year, and had one tournament to play during the break, the Slice of Life Pro-Am, in Carterville, Illinois.

I knew I was going to play well. The Slice of Life is held every year at Crab Orchard Golf Club, about an hour and a half from St. Louis. I was so excited to get there that I got a speeding ticket in Southern Illinois, doing ninety-three miles per hour in a sixty-five-mile-an-hour zone. I was in such a hurry to warm up once I arrived at the course that I slammed my head into the door of my trunk as it was opening. The knot on the side of head was so large I couldn't wear a hat for the entire day. But it didn't slow down my golf game. Bipolar disorder gets your mind moving so fast that even the simplest of tasks, such as getting your golf clubs out of the trunk, can become dangerous.

I bogeyed the first hole but followed that opening blunder with eight birdies to post a score of 67, putting with my eyes closed. It was the first time that I ever used my new technique in a tournament and it worked. If I didn't pour a putt into the hole, it lipped out or stopped only inches away. I earned a check for $1,650.

The Pro-Am paycheck, combined with the money I made caddying for Jimmy Liu, was enough to cover the cost of the Q-School entry fee. I paid $2,500 to enter the newly created Q-School Pre-Qualifying Stage. There are so many good players trying to qualify for the PGA Tour now that the tour had to add another stage to the Q-School in 2010, making it four stages instead of three.

I had two weeks to practice my ass off, get into the gym, to give myself a good chance of advancing through the qualifying process. I was playing so well that I had no doubt that this was my year: I was going to get my PGA Tour card.

Fourteen days to Q-School.

* * *

It was Labor Day weekend, and I was on the loose for a three-day weekend holding a new stash of Adderall and looking for a bar to begin my assault on Seagram's whiskey. I felt like Superman. I was playing amazing golf, I had earned enough money to pay my own way to Q-School, and I was taking my lithium every day—I felt impervious to any bipolar struggles.

I kicked off Friday night at my cousin's bar, The Pour House, ordering my customary 7 and 7. I finished it in a matter of seconds and ordered a Bud Light. I slammed the beer so quickly that the bottle was still ice-cold when I pulled out my wallet and left $30—way too much money for two drinks.

I didn't see anyone at The Pour House that I recognized, so I went out-side and sat in my car. I was bored, which is a dangerous state for the manic mind. I began blaring an Eminem CD and formulated my next move while I contemplated what to do with my wide-open Friday night. I decided to head down to the St. Louis Riverfront and take on the Lumière casino; my car couldn't get me there fast enough.

* * *

When I finally got to the casino, the bright lights, ringing bells, and fresh oxygen in the air put me in a euphoric state of mind. I had come there to do one thing: beat the hell out of a dealer in blackjack. If I were in my right mind, I would have taken a seat at a table with other gamblers, where it would be easier to win. Instead, I found an empty table and sat down to face the dealer one-on-one. She was an attractive woman, probably in her early forties, with bleach-blond hair, half a dozen gold rings on her right hand, and four gold bracelets on her left wrist. Her face and figure reminded me of Halle Berry, but her name tag read Nancy.

"Are you still going to like me after I take all the casino's money?" I had slipped into trash-talking mode.

"Of course, child. Sit down." She smiled. "As long as you tip well." I was definitely at the right table.

After sending my Q-School entry in, I was broke. I put my last $160 on the table and asked for chips. My first bet was $50. I got blackjack on my first hand.

What to do? I doubled my next bet to $100 and won that one with a soft seventeen; the dealer busted.

My confidence was bubbling, and the mania felt magnificent. I raised my third bet to $160 and won that with twenty against the dealer's nineteen. I felt like I had just made three birdies in a row. I raised my next bet to $200.

"Keep going, child!" The dealer was on my team because for every hand I won, I tipped her two $5 chips.

My next wager was another $200. I was dealt eighteen with the dealer showing nine. Not a good spot, but I couldn't hit on the eighteen. When I stood, the dealer turned over a two. Now I was thinking, *Oh shit, if she turns over a ten or a face card next, it will break my streak.* She flipped over another two, which gave her thirteen. Her next card was a three, getting her hand up to sixteen. I was standing up at the table, hunched right on top of all the cards and squirming with every card that was dealt. Then she drew my money card: the one-eyed jack of spades. That gave her twenty-six to bust, and I took another $200 off the table and sliding her a $20

Now I was sitting at the table with approximately $1,000 in chips in front of me, and I hadn't lost a single hand.

Fuck it, I thought. I put up $500 on the next hand.

"I am rooting for you, child," she told me as she pushed her gold bracelets up toward her elbow and jingled them to make a church bell sound. She dealt me sixteen, which is a bad hand, with her showing a ten of hearts. *Fuck it* ran through my thoughts again.

"Hit me, Nancy . . . but be gentle." Any card higher than a five, and I would lose. She gave me a four of diamonds, putting me at twenty. I stood with an emphatic hand gesture. She then turned over a nine, giving her nineteen, which wasn't enough to beat my twenty. I took my winnings off the table and flipped her two $25 chips in thanks. Then I stuffed all my chips into the pockets of my blue jeans and raced toward the cashier's booth to trade them in.

"Come back, child!" Nancy yelled as I left her table. I didn't even look back. I felt like I had just robbed a bank.

The cashier gave me fourteen $100 bills after adding up the chips. I left the casino in a half jog that turned into a full sprint when I got into the parking lot. The mania was flowing like the nearby Mississippi River—easy, steady, and looking to be let loose. And now I had money to go out and drink.

* * *

I popped a celebratory Adderall as I drove out of the parking. It heightened my thirst for a cold beer. I was ready to attack downtown St. Louis for a solo-mission bar hop.

My first stop was Lucas Park. I made a beeline to the bar and ordered a bottle of Bud Select and a shot of tequila. I slammed the shot, poured the beer down my throat, and left $100 bill on the bar and walked out. The tab was $12.00.

The next venue on my mission was the Side Bar, just across the street from Lucas Park. The walk over was surreal; I felt like I was walking a foot above the pavement. I had a pocket full of dough from "robbing" the casino and I was high on my sharp golf game and Q-School entry.

This is my year to make it through Q-School.

Q-School dominated my mind most hours of the day. I wasn't so enamored with the tournament itself, but I was obsessed with the effort to improve, to constantly get better so I could play my best golf. My workouts in the gym were fierce, my short-game practice was intense, and I was making birdies in bunches.

I am preparing the right way this time.

When I walked into the Side Bar, the dark atmosphere relaxed me a little bit. I set up shop at the end of the bar and actually sat still for a good fifteen minutes, although it felt like two hours. I ordered a Red Bull, a shot of Jägermeister, and another Bud Select and texted Matt Ratz. He worked not far away.

>**Me:** *Where you at?*
>**Ratz:** *I'm at work. Come by 15. Great scenery here.* (Jim Edmonds 15 Steakhouse—15 for short—was named for legendary St. Louis Cardinals outfielder and his jersey number.)
>**Me:** *Sold.*

I asked the bartender for my tab. The total was $18.00, so—of course—I left a $100 bill under the receipt and made another beeline for my car.

I pulled up to the valet at 15 and made the exchange with the valet guy—another $100 bill—as he grabbed the keys from my hand.

When Ratz saw me walk in the door, he knew I was wasted.

"Wells!" he said, laughing and happy to see me.

"Ratzie!" I screamed and grabbed him in the classic "I-am-hammered-and-I-love-ya-man!" hug.

"How'd you get here?" Ratz asked.

"I drove," I said with a drunken smile.

"Jesus! Give me your fuckin' keys. I am calling you a cab," he took control with a smile.

Ratz brought me over to the bar, where our friend Nick Maynes was working. Maynes babysat me while Ratz called me a cab, watching me eat lemons out of the bar service tray one after another.

The cab finally showed up and Ratz put me in the backseat and handed the cab driver a $50 bill so the cabby would get me home. As soon as the door closed, I blacked out.

* * *

I woke up in a jail cell, lying on the freezing cement floor. Bars separated me from a vacant hallway. To my right was a single twin bed with a thin, pink-and-white striped mattress atop the screen of the metal box spring. I turned over and looked behind me to find a black video camera watching every move I made.

When I stood up, I noticed that I was only wearing my blue jeans. No shirt, no socks, no shoes, no belt, no watch, no cell phone—nothing. All the cash I had won at the casino was gone, too. My mania had significantly calmed, but I had a migraine induced by the potpourri of different alcohols in my system. The booze was leaking out of me in a grimy sweat, and my hair was greasy from it.

Then I started freaking out.

I worried that I had hurt or killed someone. The bipolar mind always defaults to the worst-case scenario. The trick for me is to let that scenario flow out and replace it with the best case. Substituting thoughts can make the worst case disappear.

I allowed my theory of hurting someone else to consume my brain while I tossed the mattress all over the cell. I twirled that mattress into the bars as if shaking out a dirty rug. I threw the mattress at the camera in the corner like a giant, rectangular Frisbee. Tears joined the sweat on my face. It was insanity, live on closed-circuit TV.

Where the fuck am I? How did I get here? Who's watching me on that camera?

Eventually I got tired, put the mattress on the floor, and lay on my back while I stared at the camera with my best poker face. I rolled over on my stomach and prayed that I hadn't hurt anyone. My memory was completely blank from the moment I got into the cab until I woke up in that cell. I had no idea what time—or even what day—it was. There were no windows in the cell, so I couldn't tell if it was light or dark outside. I just lay there. It could have been ten minutes or ten hours until finally I heard keys clinking. A police officer dressed in all black unlocked the door.

"It's time to come out, Mr. Wellington." He said quietly, but not making eye contact. I followed him down the hall to a room with six televisions and a console that looked like it belonged inside the *Millennium Falcon*. There was a plastic bag on the counter filled with my shoes, wallet, shirt, belt, and white Cardinals ball cap.

As I put my wallet in my pocket and my hat on my pounding head, I looked to my left to see my brother standing in an open doorway. The look on his face was pure disgust. I had never seen him so mad.

"Put your shirt on, and let's go, asshole," he barked at me.

"Good to see you, too, Kev," I told him as I wrestled my T-shirt over my head.

I followed him down a short hallway to a door that led outside into the parking lot. I was at the Richmond Heights Police Station, and it was daytime—a beautiful day, actually, with bright, blue skies and a temperature in the 70s. As we walked through the parking lot, I noticed my dad's navy blue Jeep Cherokee in one of the parking spaces ahead of us.

Fuck . . . Dad is gonna light me up.

But he didn't. He looked frightened and didn't say anything. My brother didn't hold back though.

"What the fuck is wrong with you, Michael? When are you gonna grow up?" My brother is seven years younger than me.

I didn't say a word. I just put my head back to nurse the hangover and closed my eyes. Awkward silence filled the car. Finally, we stopped. I opened my eyes to see that we were at the emergency room at Barnes–Jewish Hospital.

You have to be kidding me—here again? . . . Fuck it. Let's go in here and see where this leads.

* * *

I didn't even put up a fight. I wasn't manic anymore; I was depressed. All the natural depressants in the alcohol from the night before had me moving slowly, and I didn't have the energy to argue with anyone.

My dad flipped on the hazard lights of his Jeep and parked right in front of the emergency room doors. He opened the back door to grab my file folder before going into the hospital.

My file was pretty thick by this point. I had had a handful of hospital stays, and my parents kept a file with dates, the details of my previous treatment, and insurance information. One of the advantages of suffering from mental illness is that you get moved to the front of the line in the emergency room—no waiting.

I followed a policeman to a secluded basement room. I stared at the small of his back and got lost in the Carolina blue of his shirt while I followed him. Finally, we reached our destination. It was a small hallway, no more than fifteen feet long, with two doors on each side. He escorted me into the first door on the left. Another all white room—white everywhere: white floors, white walls, white ceiling, white camera mounted over the white door, and a small two-by-two-foot window looking out into the freedom of the vacant white hallway.

Inside there was only one item: a twin mattress with no box spring in a white sheet on the floor. My mania turned to anger when the door closed behind me. I was mad at my brother and my dad for putting me back in the hospital. I thought I was just suffering from a bad hangover, and if I just had a moment to lie down on the couch and watch football, eating pizza, I would be back to normal by dinnertime. My mania was back and out in the open.

The truth was that the cops at Richmond Heights saved my life by getting me off the street. My dad and brother had read the police report and knew this wasn't just a drunk night out. I had blacked out from mixing all of that alcohol, but my bipolar mind was so strong that it stayed awake while my rational mind slept. I don't remember any of what happened: don't recall the cop car, don't know whether I had cuffs on—nothing. The police report, which I've included here, sheds direct light on what happened and how the bipolar mind can be dangerous.

Richmond Heights Police Department

We had been advised by dispatch of a shirtless man staggering in the roadway and nearly being struck by traffic. He had poor balance and appeared intoxicated by manner and speech.

At one point in the interview, he requested that the police shoot him due to the physical harm he might cause to himself.

He was taken into custody for disorderly conduct: by public intoxication and walking in a roadway.

Wellington was conveyed to this station and booked. During the booking process, he removed all of his clothes and made claims of being a demon.

Respectfully submitted,
PO Milward

That was not really me asking the cops to shoot me and claiming to be a demon. That was the disorder, literally trying to have me killed.

So it was back to Barnes–Jewish Hospital for another turn around the psychiatric ward. I was thirty-two years old—adult enough by far to wonder why this kept happening to me. *I have been taking my medicine, how can I be here? Everything is supposed to be okay if I take my medicine!*

I had cemented into my mind that if I took my medicine every day, my life would run smoothly, but the fight against bipolar disorder isn't won only by proper medication. It requires other tools—a healthy diet, an established routine—to keep bipolar at bay (see the Fourteen Clubs at the end of the chapter). At this point in my life, I believed that if I took my lithium every day, I could ignore the other important aspects of creating a healthy lifestyle. I was wrong.

The alcohol from the previous evening had negated the effects of my lithium and turned me into that demon. I had been able to keep the mania reasonably at bay because of the sober week caddying at the US Amateur, but a night of binge drinking had pushed me over the edge.

While lying on the mattress in the white room, I committed to never drinking again. The exhaustion of the previous fourteen hours overtook me, and I passed out again.

* * *

When I awoke, frustration poured over me as I sat up to see where I was. It was night, and I was now in a two-bed suite on the fifteenth floor with my own bathroom and windows overlooking Forest Park and the heart of St. Louis. It had been four years since I had seen a room like this, and I thought I'd never see it again.

No way I am here right now . . . I gotta get out of here before Q-School . . . I need to practice . . . What day is it? How many days until Q-School?

I walked out into the hall and realized that I was wearing a royal blue hospital gown with no underwear. *Who took my underwear off?* A sense of violation flowed through my mind and down my spine.

The linoleum was freezing on my bare feet. The entire floor was silent and dark, the only light on the floor shining from the nurses' station. I walked toward the light and came across a man in a lab coat sitting at the nurses' station, playing solitaire on his computer. He looked like Christopher Walken with gray hair, and I could smell cigarette smoke on him.

"What time is it?" I asked him.

"2:22," he informed me without looking up from his card game.

"Make a wish. 2:22. Make a wish," I responded. It was the first thing that came to my mind, and it produced an awkward silence.

"What day is it?" I asked to break the silence.

"Sunday morning," he said in another dead tone.

"No, sir. What is today's date?"

"Sunday, September 5, 2010, and it's now 2:23 in the morning." He finally looked up at me like a parent looks at an annoying six-year-old. I always liked Christopher Walken, but this guy was an asshole.

Eleven days to Q-School.

As I walked back to my room, I found a window that looked out over the city. I scanned all the familiar buildings in the distance. If I was on the outside, I would have been right in the thick of all of those lights; 2:30 in the morning was prime time in my world.

After a few hours of sedatives and needles in my arm, I was calm, but I cried quietly for the loss of my freedom. I wanted to use every free minute to make my golf better and being in the hospital was cutting into my time. I fell asleep with tears running down my cheeks.

* * *

My dad visited the next day and brought bad news.

"Michael, you can't go to San Antonio for Q-School. They want you to stay in here for eleven days, and that obviously overlaps with San Antonio."

I was silent. All the good work that I had put in during the course of the year didn't matter anymore. All the practice on my short game, all the traveling around the country, all the experimentation to finally learn that I putt better with my eyes closed, all the sessions in the gym making my body stronger and more flexible—all of it for nothing. I would have to withdraw from the tournament. My dad had the paperwork with him. As I filled it out, I became sick to my stomach; my belly was bubbling, and I even dry-heaved twice as I signed my name. I also had to prepare a separate letter to the PGA Tour, stating that the reason for my withdrawal was "complications with bipolar disorder."

I knew this situation hurt Dad, too. He knew how well I was playing, and he is my biggest fan. I finished all the paperwork, handed it to him, and went back to my room to lie on my stomach, trying to keep from vomiting. I would have eleven more days to let this feeling eat me up. The only silver lining was that I would get my $2,500 entry fee back.

* * *

As typical for my stays at Barnes, I had many visitors. My best friend Michael Eveler came to see me.

"What happened? Did you stop taking your medication?" he asked.

"No," I said. "I haven't missed a day taking my lithium since 2006."

"So what was it?"

"Too much booze," I told him. "The doctors are telling me that the amount of alcohol in my system completely negated all the positive effects of my medicine. I can't drink anymore; I am done with it."

I had learned my lesson during the hospitalization time and made a determined effort to go to all the group therapy sessions during this stay. Social workers led two or three groups a day to help the patients work through different issues. I never missed a music therapy group and lost myself in the music. I listened to Dave Matthews, the Counting Crows, the Beatles, Pearl Jam, and U2. The music worked again to help drag me out of depression, if only for forty-five minutes a day. This was my first taste of how important therapy—music therapy, in particular—can be in combatting bipolar disorder. Therapy was so effective that I made them part of the Fourteen Clubs.

I was lonely in the hospital, so I called Hope. Hers was one of the few numbers I could remember by heart. She didn't answer, so I left a voice mail.

Two men that I greatly respect surprised me with a visit: Jay Eveler, Michael's dad, and Greg Vitello, Tony's dad. Their presence showed how much they truly cared about my well-being, even if I hadn't.

"Hey Mike, this place isn't exactly the Ritz," Greg greeted me, with a smart-ass grin. "Let's sit down and talk."

Jay had watched me grow up and had been my coach in many different sports. He knew that bringing Greg to the hospital would get my attention. Greg had won more than 700 games and six state championships coaching soccer at DeSmet Jesuit High School, and had led the school to a state championship in baseball, as well. I had been a part of his 1995 Missouri State Championship soccer team; I didn't always agree with his choices as a coach, but we won, and that's all that I cared about.

"Michael, we know you have been taking your medicine, but you have to stop with the drinking," Jay started the intervention.

"Do you think you have a problem, Mike?" Greg asked with a straight face.

"I can tell you that I am not the type of alcoholic that needs it as soon as I wake up in the morning," I explained, "but I struggle with having only a few drinks in an evening. I believe I am a binge-drinking alcoholic. I know I have no choice anymore. I have to quit. I can do it."

After Jay and Greg left, I checked my voice mail. I had a message from Hope.

"Mike, I heard you had to go back. I am so sorry. Call me whenever you want, and if I can answer, I will. I am gonna try and come by in the next few days. Take care."

I hadn't heard from or seen Hope in a year and a half, and she was right there when I needed her. She showed up at the hospital the next day.

"I don't even want to talk about how you got here, but when you get out and you need someone to talk to, you can talk to me," she said.

The rest of her visit was filled with laughter and small talk, mostly focused on making fun of me for winding up back in the loony bin. I made fun of myself because I knew that although I was capable of handling the disorder, it had fooled me again.

"I am gonna go, but call me when you get out," she said as she kissed me on the cheek.

Damn, she looked good!

* * *

Two days after getting out of Barnes in the fall of 2010, I competed at the Gateway Masters at Bogey Hills Country Club. My friend Angel Walters, the tournament director, got me in at the last minute when she learned that I was out of the hospital.

I had wanted so badly to play while I was locked up, and I was under the illusion that I would pick right up where I had left off twelve days earlier. In my last precommitment tournament round, I posted a 67 putting with my eyes closed and hardly missed a shot. But after eleven days of my body chemistry being turned upside down, my balance and rhythm were gone.

I knew on the first hole that it would be a long day. Everything was moving too slowly. The clubs felt heavy in my hands. My touch around the greens was oafish. Putts over ten feet were an adventure. I had been robbed of all my skill and confidence in just two weeks. Two weeks earlier, I had never been sharper with my game, but now the game seemed foreign.

I shot 84 in the first round, but I was so happy to be out on the golf course. It was the happiest 84 that I have ever had in my life. I returned the next day and posted a 77. Those were two scores I'd typically be embarrassed by, but I didn't care. I was just happy to be back in society.

Three hundred forty-nine days to Q-School.

THE FOURTEEN CLUBS

My alcohol-fueled depression led to further self-medication with Adderall, which led to a dangerous cycle of mania and more drinking. Only another hospital stay—with individual, group, and music therapy—and the encouragement of my support system to stop drinking were able to pull me out of it, if only temporarily.

9

THE FINAL EPISODE

The best way to change something that's around you,
something you don't like, is to change yourself.
—Eddie Vedder

BY THE END of September in 2010, I needed a new plan after what I believed would be the final hospital stay in my bipolar career.

My financial angel appeared at just that moment.

A close and financially successful friend of mine had been monitoring my golf game during the summer of 2010 and knew I had missed Q-School. He came to with me with a deal I couldn't refuse—a credit card to cover tournament expenses until April. His financial support allowed me seven months to chase the PGA Tour, with only two conditions: I couldn't drink and he didn't want anyone to ever know that he had helped me. I would pay him back with 75 percent of any winnings that I received during his sponsorship.

More things slowly started to go my way. My $2,500 refund from the PGA Tour from withdrawing from Q-School arrived. That plus the backing from Mr. Anonymous helped me see a new beginning. I decided to head west to play in what the PGA Tour calls Monday Qualifiers. On the way, I stopped in Fort Worth, Texas, to visit my old partner in crime Tony Vitello. He had been lured away from the University of Missouri's baseball program by Texas Christian University to be the school's new director of recruiting and hitting instructor.

While visiting Tony at TCU, I met Brian Cain, a mental health angel of sorts. Cain is a peak performance expert, a mental conditioning coach, an educational leader, and the author of *Toilets, Bricks, Fish Hooks and Pride* and *So What, Next Pitch!* He understands great performance and poor performance and why they each happen. In addition to working with the TCU baseball program, he works with other NCAA Division I college baseball programs, such as Baylor, Coastal Carolina, Oregon State, the University of Mississippi, and Vanderbilt. He also works with the Vermont hockey program, the Auburn University swimming and diving team, the University of Alabama women's softball team, and the Yale University field hockey program. His most notable work is coaching three-time Ultimate Fighting World Championship winner Georges St-Pierre. Cain is a master of the mental game.

Tony thought that Cain could really help my mental game as a golfer, so we attended his sports psychology seminar for the TCU players. In life, I have met two types of people: toxic people, who suck positive energy out of any situation, and energizing people, who constantly give off a positive energy. Cain is an energizer. In his seminar he was like the Energizer Bunny of positive energy. Confidence and mental tenacity radiated from him.

I picked his brain every second that we were together, and he brought to light four very important keys to getting the best performance out of my golf game. More importantly he gave me keys to living a healthy life: conscious choice, routine, adequate sleep, and a healthy diet. His help led directly to my creation of the Fourteen Clubs and to writing this book to share inspiration with a wider audience.

"Mike, it is your choice," Cain said. "You can choose to be confident, or you can choose to be weak minded. The only person who can decide between those two things is you. When you stand behind a golf shot, you can choose to tell yourself that you will attack your target, or you can choose to tell yourself that this shot will go into a water hazard. It is your choice every time, so pick one. The choice is obvious."

He then talked with me about the importance of routine. I needed a strong preshot routine before hitting any golf shot. I had a subconscious but informal routine already, but he taught me how to use my conscious mind to go through the specific steps of my routine and then allow my subconscious mind to take over after the routine was complete. At the time, I thought implementing this routine would only apply to my golf; however, I began to employ a similar routine to battle bipolar disorder and have had great success with it.

He stressed the importance of sleep. I had never really felt like I needed much sleep to function well, but that mind-set, coupled with my bipolar disorder, stole hundreds of hours of precious sleep from me over the years. Cain told me how important sleep and rest are to achieving peak performance and described how fatigue can be just as detrimental as negative thinking.

He also gave me a brand new diet to try, which included more water, more fruit, more vegetables, more protein, and—my favorite—more crunchy peanut butter. At the time, my diet consisted mostly of cheeseburgers, pizza, and chocolate milkshakes.

Cain is a genius in mental performance, and the timing of our meeting could not have been more ideal: I was fresh from my hospital stay and vulnerable to a bout of depression; when I was around Cain, any depressive symptoms evaporated. He gave my positive mind the wake-up call that I sorely needed. He encouraged me to plan for success instead of focusing on fear of failure. Cain taught me how important it is to surround yourself with positive and uplifting people.

With Cain's philosophy burned into my brain, I left Fort Worth for the California desert.

* * *

I planned to spend November and December of 2010 in one of my favorite places on earth, La Quinta, California, working on my new mental approach while practicing for the PGA Tour Monday Qualifiers, which would begin in early 2011.

The first tournament I entered was the two-day Golden State Tour event at Oak Valley Golf Club, in Beaumont, California. Using Cain's advice and swing tips from Tom Stickney, the director of golf instruction at Big Horn Golf Club, I put together two strong rounds, firing 69–72, to make the cut and a miniscule paycheck. The good play in those rounds was also aided by my caddie, Loudan Steffes. Our banter was thick with movie quotes, and it felt good to be back in my element with a great caddie. It was real golf: a player and his caddie taking apart a golf course step by step. I was back on track after a course adjustment that was changing my life.

I began to explore the idea of gratitude. I had spent most of my life thinking of the things that I didn't have but wanted. By focusing my thoughts on gratitude I turned my attention toward all the good things that I already had. Instead of acting sour because I wasn't on the PGA Tour yet, I locked in on all the little things that I had in my life that normally go unnoticed. I began keeping a gratitude journal. Every morning, I sat in the backyard at a black plastic picnic table and wrote fifteen to twenty things for which I was grateful—things like my car and the freedom it gave me, my iPod and music, and the ability to walk without any physical issues. I was grateful for the music and the weather (which was easy in Southern California), and even the bipolar energy racing through my body. I used gratitude to make a mental shift from feeling empty to feeling full, and it helped my attitude both on and off the golf course.

* * *

I needed to find someone to split gas and hotel expenses with for my West Coast swing. I called my friend Chris Naegel, one of the most naturally gifted professional golfers that I have ever met. The guy can carry his driver 320 yards in the air achieving the type of length off the tee that makes people stop and stare. I had traveled with him on the NGA Hooters Tour and enjoyed being around him. I also called my friend Drew Pranger, who had turned professional earlier in 2010 and was practicing in Florida.

"Get on a plane and come out here." I instructed.

"In," he replied. It was the easiest sales job of all time.

I had traveled with Pranger the summer before, from Maine down the East Coast. He was familiar with my last manic episode, so he could keep an eye on me.

Naegel and Pranger flew into Ontario International, in Southern California, and we headed to San Diego for the Farmers Insurance Open at Torrey Pines, the first Monday Qualifier of the 2011 season.

In order to get into the Monday Qualifier, we had to make the cut in a prequalifying round on the Friday before. That week's prequalifier was held at an awful Johnny Miller–designed golf course called Maderas, only a few miles from the Pacific Ocean and not too far from downtown San Diego. It is such a bad golf course that they allowed the players to drive carts up and down its steep hills, mounds, and slopes. In real golf tournaments, players walk with caddies; they don't ride golf carts. None of us advanced through to the Monday Qualifier, and we all agreed the golf course was a complete nightmare.

We packed up my Honda and headed east. A five-hour drive landed us in Phoenix for the qualifying of the Waste Management Phoenix Open. The prequalifier for Naegel and me was held at McCormick Ranch, in the heart of Scottsdale. Pranger was assigned to qualify at Lone Tree, a forty-five-minute drive away.

The McCormick Ranch prequalifier was the most poorly run golf event that I have ever played in. It took my group four hours and twelve minutes to complete the front nine. Pranger, who teed off at Lone Tree at the same time I teed at McCormick, returned when I still had two holes left to play. Pranger missed advancing by a single shot at Lone Tree, Naegel missed by three at McCormick Ranch, and I missed by a mile.

After that disappointment, some of my depressive symptoms returned. I felt down and blamed my symptoms on the lithium. I still didn't have enough respect for the disorder to realize the root of my symptoms, so I went off my medication in the hopes of shedding the depression. I told myself I was going to take a little break from the meds. Just a little, tiny, ever-so-small break.

* * *

After we all missed qualifying in Scottsdale, Naegel and Pranger headed east to see their families and I made my way back to L.A. to prepare for the Northern Trust Open qualifier. I got in some good practice with my friend Greg Forrester at both Hillcrest and Lakeside Country Clubs and then drove south of L.A. for the prequalifier at Los Serranos Country Club.

I excitedly recruited Loudan Steffes to caddie for me again and I looked forward to playing real golf, walking with a great caddie not riding carts or any such bullshit.

Unfortunately, we were bogged down by our playing partner, a young kid who posted 96. We spent all day looking for his golf balls and holding up the entire golf course. I posted 73 and missed the cut by five strokes.

I had 2,687 miles between me and the next Monday Qualifier, in

Florida. I did the drive by myself, stopping in Fort Worth and Mobile on the way, and joining forces again with Pranger in Naples.

Pranger has a home in Naples, where he is a member at Larry Bird's course, The Hideout. This place has the fastest Bermuda grass greens that I had ever seen. They ran thirteen on the stimpmeter (a tool that measures the green's speed) every day that I played there; the greens were greased lightning. The Hideout was a great place to work on my short game. Pranger, who had been to the Dave Pelz short-game schools, taught me dozens of different shots and theories he had learned from Pelz. I also took a lesson on my swing from former Champions Tour player Terry Archer. He taught me how to move my body a little differently when I played my shots, and his technique raised my play to another level.

After playing and practicing for a week at The Hideout, I drove across the state to West Palm Beach to play the Honda Classic Pre-Qualifier with a secret weapon back on my bag. My old bagman, Johnny Mullin, was working at the Everglades Club in Palm Beach at that time and took the day off to carry my clubs. Mullin had been through the trenches with me at three different Q-Schools and countless other events. I was pumped when he told me he got the day off work to loop for me at PGA National's Estates Course.

We arrived to the eighteenth hole at two under for the day and I felt like we needed one more birdie to qualify. The eighteenth hole at The Estates Course is a very reachable par five that measures 532 yards. I snap-hooked my tee shot into the left trees and was lucky to even land in bounds. I would be forced to lay up from the trees on the left. I played a low, sweeping hook around the low-hanging branches and got the ball onto the fairway. I had 138 yards to the hole and needed to hit this shot close in order for a realistic chance at a birdie putt.

"Take dead aim, Michael," Mullin reminded me.

I locked in on the flagstick and fired a hard-pitching wedge at the target, but I pulled the shot left of the hole leaving twenty-five feet left to make birdie—not a very good shot with a wedge in my hand.

"Fuck, Johnny. I pulled it bad," I confessed.

"You can make that putt; it's gonna be uphill," Mullin reminded me.

There are no scoreboards at the Monday Qualifiers, so we had no idea whether we needed to be aggressive or smart with that putt. It was possible that I could just two-putt from this spot and still qualify, but it was just as likely that I would need to make the putt in order to qualify. I played it to break about a foot from left to right as it died at the hole. I went through my preshot routine and buried the putt for a clutch birdie to end the round.

That putt gave me back some confidence that I hadn't felt for a long time, but we had to wait another six hours before finding out if we qualified. Mullin went back to work at the Everglades Club, and I tried to stay busy until we learned our fate on the Internet.

Mullin called me with the news around dinnertime: "Missed by one."

Silence. My body felt heavy again. We each rewound the day in our heads, thinking about different places we could have saved that extra shot.

"Well, if you do this long enough, this is gonna happen," I admitted.

"Great playing today, Pro. You were solid all day long. Keep playing well, and good things will happen." Mullin built me up.

That round wasn't a failure for me at all; it was positive momentum. I had played well all day and birdied the last hole when I absolutely had to do it. I had played a professional round of golf.

I picked Pranger up in Naples, and we headed to Tampa to the Monday Qualifier for the Transitions Championship. I would caddie for Pranger at his qualifier, and he would caddie for me at mine, because we were playing the same golf course on different days. I was his swing teacher, and he was my short-game instructor. Pranger was a great caddie, too; he adopted the Bones–Mickelson style of teamwork: honesty and firm decision making for each shot.

I missed my qualifier by two strokes. I got a little too aggressive late in my round, and it cost me. Pranger played well at his qualifier but missed by one shot. He headed back to Naples, and I received a very interesting offer from my friend Jimmy Moore.

* * *

Jimmy and I grew up together at Westborough in St. Louis, and he was about ten years older than me. I caddied for him twice when he won the club championship at Westborough.

Jimmy knew that I was struggling financially to keep my golf career alive. My contract with Mr. Anonymous was up soon and I needed a new financial angel, so Jimmy set me up with a guy he knew about two hours southeast of Tampa. If I played well in front of this guy he would be my new sponsor; I didn't have a dime to my name at this point, just Mr. Anonymous's credit card good for only another few weeks.

The new benefactor hosted me at the Red Stick Golf Club, in Vero Beach. We had breakfast in the men's locker room.

As soon as I sat down to breakfast, he told me, "My firm just closed a lawsuit for over $300 million."

I played along. "Oh yeah? How much of that goes into your pocket?"

Without missing a beat, he told me, "Around twenty-five million dollars." Then he washed his bacon down with a tall glass of Florida orange juice.

Sheesh.

Now my adrenaline was racing; asking this guy, who just pocketed twenty-five million dollars, for $30,000 didn't seem unreasonable if I played well. $30,000 would only give me another eight months to play, but I needed something to keep me going.

Red Stick is a wonderful Rees Jones design that fit my eye right away. We decided to play a simple $10 match, but I needed to play well to get this guy's attention. The first hole was a perfect start for me. I hit the tee shot into a fairway bunker and then stuffed a 145-yard eight-iron shot to two feet for a tap-in birdie. I made three more birdies on the front nine and was four under at the turn. On the back nine, I added five more birdies, including four in a row to end the round with an exclamation-point chip-in birdie on the eighteenth hole to set a course record of 64. Needless to say, I won the bet and got the lawyer's attention. We exchanged contact info, and I sent him a detailed proposal but never heard back from him.

I guess he must have expected me to shoot 59.

* * *

When I left Vero Beach, I headed for Lafayette, Louisiana, for the Chitimacha Classic Monday Qualifier on the Web.com Tour. But I was also going to meet Hope in New Orleans on the evening of the qualifier. Hope and

I had been calling and texting each other ever since my last hospital stay and it felt like we were coming back into each other's lives for the better.

When I got to Lafayette, I stayed with my college teammate Burt Cestia. I'd stay with Burt on Sunday night, qualify on Monday, go pick up Hope on Monday night, and bring her back to Lafayette for the tournament. She had never seen me play, and I really wanted her to feel the energy at a golf tournament.

At the Chitimacha qualifier, I made a mistake that I had vowed would never happen again: I didn't get a caddie and carried my own clubs. I played the first fifteen holes in one under par and then ran out of gas. I shot 73; I needed 67 to get into the event. The silver lining was that Hope and I would have more time in New Orleans.

I raced to see her after turning in my scorecard. We had dinner at a sushi joint off Bourbon Street. She looked at me strangely but didn't say anything at dinner. At breakfast, she challenged me: "Have you been taking your medicine?"

I chewed a slice of bacon and answered, "Not for a while—been about a month or so since I took any."

"I can tell." She knew me like no one else.

"I just started feeling bad in Phoenix and decided the medication was bringing me down," I explained.

"Mike, you have to take it," she said as tears filled her big beautiful brown eyes.

I didn't like to see her cry, but I had been playing better golf since going off the lithium and hadn't felt depressive since my time in Phoenix, so there was no way I was going to allow her to convince me.

That is a problem with the bipolar mind. Its first instinct is to refuse help or to listen to anyone else. The bipolar mind can do it all itself; it's invincible.

But that's bullshit.

People need people; it's just that simple. I would later learn how to push through the thoughts of stubborn self-sufficiency to being able to accept help. Hope knew how important it was for me to take my medication, but I didn't want to listen to her. To her credit, she persisted for the rest of our time in New Orleans.

After a ten-hour drive from New Orleans back to St. Louis, I dropped her off. We parted in an awkward silence. I drove home, but she called me about half an hour later. Hope finally got through the bipolar bravado when she told me what I most feared.

"Mike, I can't be with you if you don't take your medicine."

I stood in my bedroom in front of the television in disbelief.

"Seriously?"

"Yes. I won't do it," she insisted.

My first instinct was bipolar defensiveness: *Fuck her.* "Ok, Hope, whatever you say," I said, in a sarcastic and irritating tone.

"Call me when you get back on your medicine," she said and hung up on me.

I sat down on my bed, my anger swelling; then it hit me. Maybe she was right. I am going back on the medicine. Or maybe try a new medicine. It could be time for a fresh start.

* * *

Hope had convinced me, but I didn't call her back. I made plans for an appointment with Dr. Cloninger. I needed to pick his brain about this medication predicament.

"Doc, about five weeks ago, I stopped taking my lithium."

"Any particular reason?"

"I was feeling low. I was out in the sunshine of the western United States and felt depressed. It made no sense to me."

"Michael, that is the disorder, not the lithium," he explained.

"Should I go back on the lithium, or do you have something else I can try? And remember, I can't take the Depakote because it makes me throw up."

"I can offer lamotrigine, which is also used to treat epilepsy," he offered.

"Well, I have had success with lithium before, so I'll stick with it. Let's hold off on the new stuff," I told him.

"Michael, I can only recommend that you take the medication. At the end of the day, it is your choice."

"I'm in, Doc. I know I need to take it. I don't want to end up in the hospital ever again."

I went back on the lithium at the beginning of April, but I kept my distance from Hope for some reason. Mr. Anonymous's sponsorship had expired, and I was back in St. Louis. I would have to hustle to save enough money in time for Q-School, so I went back to caddying at Old Warson, I became a courier for my dad's printing company again, I gave as many golf lessons as possible, and I played as many money games as I could. Gambling on the golf course had paid many of my bills, so I found money games for another revenue stream.

In June, I tied the course record at Glen Echo Country Club, with a 63. At the end of June, on Father's Day, I played a round with my dad, my brother, and Drew Pranger at Westborough Country Club. On the eighteenth tee that day, my dad noticed I had selected a three wood to play my tee shot. Normally, I always hit a driver on Westborough's home hole.

"Why are you hitting three wood here?" he questioned me.

"I need to get this ball in the fairway; if I hole out my second shot here, I will shoot 59." My brother and Pranger knew I was having a great round, but Dad had gotten lost in his own game and didn't realize I was going low. I found the fairway and played a nine iron to fifteen feet, but missed the birdie putt and tapped in for a 61. It was the best Father's Day gift that I ever gave to my dad. He loved the game so much and was ecstatic to see me playing so well and being so healthy.

* * *

By the end of July, I had saved enough money for Q-School and put together a tournament schedule to sharpen my skills.

The first event on my schedule was the Colorado Open, a Monday Qualifier in Denver. I had to play a one-round qualifying event at Legacy Ridge the Friday before. My good friend Rob Faber lived in Denver and caddied for me.

I played solid all day except for one hiccup—a sloppy bogey on the tenth hole. I made birdies at eleven and fifteen and a slippery twelve-foot par-saving putt on number eighteen to post a 72, but I missed qualifying by one shot again.

I had eleven days before my next event, in Kansas, so I called my old caddie friends Loudan Steffes and Chad Brenegen who were both working at the Rock Creek Cattle Company in Deer Lodge, Montana. They invited me to come practice at the Rock Creek golf course when they heard that I had some time to kill. It is a devilish Tom Doak design with a top-notch practice facility. The drive from Denver to Deer Lodge is about ten hours, but by this time in my life it seemed like a reasonable commute.

Loudan got me a couple of high-paying caddie jobs while I was in Big Sky Country, and I spent every moment between them working on my short game. I would turn on my iPod and get lost in the practice, sometimes for nine hours straight. I worked on every shot you can imagine from 120 yards and into the hole: full wedges, knock-down wedges, flop shots, easy bunker shots, impossible bunker shots, bump-and-run shots, pitch shots, short putts, long putts, and everything in between. I had the best practice I'd ever seen during those seven days in Deer Lodge, and I was healthy and free of mania. My putts were diving in the hole, my chips were dancing all around the hole, and my sand shots were behaving exactly how I visualized them.

I left Montana for Garden City, Kansas, to play in the Southwest Kansas Pro-Am, which PGA Tour player Gary Woodland won while he was cutting his teeth in golf's minor leagues. My good friend John Kelly was playing in the event and had arranged free on-course housing for us with a wonderful family in Garden City.

The tournament took place at two different golf courses: the Golf Club at Southwind and Buffalo Dunes. My first round was at Southwind, and I posted a sloppy 72 and missed many opportunities. I would have to go low in the second round just to make the cut. I opened my second round at Buffalo Dunes with a birdie on the first hole, added another birdie on my eighth hole, and finished the front nine at two under par for the day.

A few birdies on the back nine and we are good.

I birdied ten, eleven, and twelve to move to five under for the day.

Forget making the cut, I thought. *We are gonna win this golf tournament!*

On the par-five thirteenth hole, the golf gods challenged me. The hole would be easy to reach in two shots, and the wind was helping. I split the fairway with a long drive and only had a six-iron shot left to the green. I played a beautiful right-to-left drawing shot that started out over the right green-side bunker and hooked onto the green; my ball finished twenty feet from the hole giving me a very realistic chance for an eagle and move me to seven under for the day.

As I walked down the fairway after playing my second shot, I found a golf ball at the edge of the right side of the fairway sitting up against where the fairway turned into deep rough. It was my ball.

One of my playing partners had played a provisional ball after his tee shot looked to be out of bounds to the left of the fairway. His original ball turned out to be in bounds after all, so he played it and forgot to pick up the provisional ball. I was so locked into my round and my momentum that I played the wrong ball in the fairway and, consequently, had to call a two-stroke penalty on myself. I went from having a great chance for eagle to making a bogey six. I was beyond frustrated walking off the thirteenth green.

I scrambled to make par on the next three holes while trying to regain my momentum. I made a costly bogey on seventeen and felt like I needed a birdie at the last hole to make the cut. This was nothing new, and I was enjoying the adrenaline.

The final hole at Buffalo Dunes was a short par four. You had to play a draw shot off the tee to get the ball in the fairway. You could also cut a corner down the left side of the hole and try and reach the green with your tee shot. I chose a one iron and played a beautiful low draw around the corner that found the fairway. Eighty-seven yards left to the hole. I played my fifty-eight-degree wedge to within two feet of the hole for the tap-in birdie to post a 68. I was in one of the last groups of the day, and when I got to the scoreboard, I learned that I made the cut exactly on the number.

The final two rounds were lackluster—two 72s—but I was excited to see that I could still make birdies when it mattered most, late in a round. I left Garden City with a small paycheck. I needed every penny I could make before Q-School.

Twenty-nine days to Q-School.

I had remained sober for the entire year. I hadn't had a drop of alcohol since the previous holiday season. I was also still taking my lithium and following Cain's diet and philosophies. I had one of his beliefs written down on a piece of paper that I kept on the passenger seat of my car:

Mental toughness is a decision you make everyday when you get out of bed. Mental toughness is a lifestyle, not an event. It always went back to Cain's motto of choosing your own mind-set. No one else can choose your mind-set for you. So I chose to own my mind; my disorder would not own me. It's a choice I needed to commit to each day, and having the note next to me as I drove around the country was a constant reminder.

I noticed, as I pulled out of Garden City, I put 29,010 miles on my car in ten months of traveling. Next stop Philadelphia, the city of brotherly love.

* * *

I planned to stop in Philadelphia to visit Ryan Plower before heading to Pittsburgh for a Web.com Monday Qualifier. Plower is another friend I met while working at Andalusia. While in Philadelphia we played at Gulph Mills and Saucon Valley, and Plower helped get my game in even better shape.

When I couldn't find a caddie, I elected not to play the qualifier in Pittsburgh. Instead, I drove down to Baltimore and practiced with my friend Rod Trump at Baltimore Country Club. Looking back, I can see that I began to receive manic signals while on my way to play with Rod at the Baltimore Country Club. Even though I had a GPS system in my car, I went back and forth on the same freeway and got turned around—it was similar to my experience in Southern Illinois when I took the baseball bat to my Honda on the side of the interstate. I got to the course eventually, and we finished nine holes before rain stopped the round.

Nothing out of the ordinary happened during my round with Rod, but I was slipping into hypomania, when all my senses are in a state of heightened arousal. It really didn't get under my skin the way full-blown mania does. I could function just fine in hypomania.

After Baltimore, I had 886 miles until my next stop at home in St. Louis.

Twenty-one days until Q-School. That phrase ran through my head thousands of times during the drive.

* * *

I was still diligent about taking my lithium every morning and staying alcohol free while in St. Louis. I had two golf events to keep me sharp leading up to Q-School. The first was at Dalhousie Golf Club, just south of St. Louis, where I put together a group of guys to play a money game. It was the definition of a boy's weekend and not very well organized: There were sixteen of us divided into four foursomes, and we played simple money matches.

The excitement of the next few weeks was overriding my sense of better judgment. I had this weekend with the boys at Dalhousie, I'd practice with my dad the following weekend in St. Louis, play another money match the weekend after that at Boone Valley Golf Club, and then go to Q-School at the Golf Club of Dallas. I was pumped up and playing very good golf.

The night before we left for Dalhousie, I began climbing to the top of the hypomanic ladder. It was a standard night out in downtown St. Louis with my good friend John Carroll, whom we all call JC. He asked me to meet him for dinner at his restaurant, Lucas Park Grill. We planned to drive to Dalhousie together the following morning, so we got an early start on our boys' weekend.

On my way to dinner with JC, I bought a pair of Nike running shoes. I didn't have the money to spend on a $145 pair of shoes. I had barely been able to pay for Q-School again, and I should have been saving that money for caddie expenses or for gas and food. My impulse buy was a textbook manic signal.

JC called it a night around 11:00 p.m., but I wasn't ready to go home. I wanted to take my new Nikes for a spin around St. Louis. I got in my car and decided to head to the Central West End, which is about ten minutes west of downtown St. Louis. During the drive, the manic feeling of supreme urgency began to take over my body; I couldn't do things fast enough. I pressed the FM button on the radio for an FM station and immediately switched to an AM station. Then, after another second, I hit the button for the CD player. I'd track between songs just as quickly, listening for only a second or two before hitting another button. This continued for the entire trip. I stayed out until three in the morning, bar hopping and drinking energy drinks, which made me wired and at the crossroads of hypomania and mania. The energy drinks are just as bad as booze.

When I got back to my place, around 3:30 in the morning, I packed for Dalhousie. We were only going for one night, but I wanted to have everything in order. My clothes, my clubs, my golf shoes, and my hats were all positioned in their assigned spots in my Honda. Around four o'clock in the morning, I slipped down a few stairs and landed on the sidewalk next to my car. I got up and karate kicked the passenger side mirror clear off the car. It crashed to the pavement, cracking the mirror and sending plastic flying everywhere.

I looked around to see whether anyone had seen me, but it was four in the morning, and most people were asleep. I took the broken mirror into my apartment and left it on the kitchen counter, thinking I would get it fixed later.

When I locked my door for the evening, it was 4:15. I couldn't sleep. I watched *Slap Shot* and *Caddyshack* while I lay in my bed, and before I knew it, it was time to get to JC's house to start the trip to Dalhousie.

I left the one-mirrored Honda in his driveway, and we packed up his black SUV for the weekend. As I was loading my clubs into JC's car, I noticed JC's dog, Heisman, a big beautiful Bernese mountain dog named in honor of college football's biggest individual award. Heisman stood about four feet tall and had a gorgeous white coat, with big brown spots all over him. He caught my attention in that moment because he looked like a cartoon. I was hallucinating, though I didn't realize it in the moment. I didn't say anything to JC about it; I just hopped in the passenger seat, tilted the leather chair back, and tried to get some sleep. I was exhausted and seeing things.

The drive to Dalhousie was smooth for about forty-five minutes, until I realized that I had left my lithium on my bathroom counter and had missed taking my morning dose. I didn't ask JC to turn around. I had been off my lithium for the entire month of March and was confident that I could miss two days of medication and not have any problems.

When we arrived at the gates of Dalhousie, I felt like a kid in a candy store. The clubhouse looked like a castle. We were staying in an on-course cottage fifteen paces from the driving range. Our cottage had a full modern kitchen, stocked refrigerator, four queen-size beds, and beautiful brown leather pullout couches. It was a golf geek's dreamland.

After we checked in, I played a game with my old buddy Nick Sansone and two new friends, David Steele and Dave Gift. I met Steele and Gift earlier in the year, and we played a lot of golf together in 2011. They loved to gamble and to compete.

The first round at Dalhousie that weekend is one of the few rounds of golf that I don't remember. I can't recall a single shot that I hit that day, but no one mentioned me doing anything out of the ordinary. Of course, this seems like a red flag now.

We had dinner that night at Celebrations Restaurant, in Cape Girardeau. We told stories and made fun of each other—typical boys' night out. At the end of dinner, I snuck a shot of Captain Morgan's Private Stock rum when my guys weren't watching. I almost vomited on the bar and had a flashback to the jail cell. It was the first drink I had had in nine months, but I stopped there; I didn't consume any more alcohol. However, I was pounding energy drinks one on top of another. By midnight, I was manic, but all my friends were drunk, so no one noticed.

We left dinner and made our way to our favorite Cape Girardeau bar, The Library. This place is a single guy's dream: beautiful Midwestern women, great music, and even a back patio to enjoy the warm summer weather. I set up shop at the inside bar and continued my assault on energy drinks, churning my mania by the minute.

I chugged an entire can of energy drink and made my way out to the back patio of the bar, where I started kicking a volleyball around the lighted sand volleyball court. I kicked the ball into the net, retrieved it, and did it again. Over and over, I'd make a handful of kicks, then walk inside for another energy drink, and quickly return to my soccer sandbar. This went on for about forty-five minutes, but the boys were all busy drinking. Sansone was drunk enough to know that he shouldn't be driving, so he gave me his car keys. I wasn't drunk (the shot of rum had been four hours earlier), but I was manic and jacked up on energy drinks. I was counting down to liftoff.

"Mike, you need to drive my car back to Dalhousie because I definitely wouldn't pass a breathalyzer right now. Dave and I are going to hit this diner for some grub; you wanna drive us and eat?"

"JC is already out in your car. I will take him back to Dalhousie; you guys grab a cab and go eat, and I will see you back there later."

I walked to the parking lot and found JC passed out in the passenger seat of Nick's silver SUV.

"JC! Hahaha! JC! You ok, man?" It has always made me laugh when I see people passed out from a strong night on the town, but the mania made me especially giddy. He didn't move. "JC!" I gave him a healthy push, and he didn't budge. He was out cold.

I put his seatbelt on him, and we headed for Dalhousie. It wouldn't be more than a ten-minute drive back to our cottage, or so I thought.

I got lost trying to find I-55, and my phone was out of juice. If I could get to I-55, I could find my way back to Dalhousie without the GPS on my phone. I wound up in an abandoned area. There was no one around, no one to ask for help, and I was frustrated. I was manic, buzzed on taurine and caffeine, and I hadn't had any lithium in my system for a solid fifty hours.

I drove around for a good twenty minutes before finally seeing a sign for I-55 that would lead us to the interstate. JC hadn't moved a muscle during the entire ride. When I saw I-55, it felt as if the gates of heaven had just opened up for me. Relief ran down my spine; I knew that I could get us back to Dalhousie from there. The world felt perfect. My nerves were calming underneath all the caffeine.

And then I took a wrong turn.

I landed on I-55, just as I had intended, but headed north rather than south.

I will just flip it around at the next exit, and we will be fine.

I missed the next exit. I missed the one after that. I kept speeding north. My mind had found a new focus: I have to get JC home to St. Louis so he can be with his two-year-old son. His son needed him and I would get him there. I started to believe that if I didn't get JC home quickly, something bad was going to happen.

It wasn't Osama bin Laden. He was dead. I was glad he was dead. There was something else that coming at us, some unknown threat.

As I sped my way north on I-55, my thoughts turned dark. I couldn't shake the feeling that I was about to die. I began seeing skulls and skeletons outside the window in the starry night sky. I began fidgeting with the radio again. I would try a new station or new source of sound every two seconds. As I contemplated my impending death, JC was dead to the world next to me in the passenger seat. I began to sweat and squirm restlessly in my seat.

My arms began to cramp and tingle as I drove. The tingling felt like the sensation you get when you knock your funny bone. Sweating, arms cramping, tingling.

My legs began the same numbness and tingling as my arms. I couldn't physically drive the car anymore.

I gotta pull over, I thought, *or I am going to lose control of this car.*

So I pulled over on the right shoulder of the two-lane highway. Eighteen-wheelers whizzed past at eighty miles per hour. I got out of the car and went around to the passenger side and opened JC's door.

"JC! JC! JC!" I shoved him and yelled in his ear, but he didn't move.

Man, I hope JC is not dead because I didn't get him to St. Louis fast enough.

My mind was in orbit, and my body was trembling in a cold grimy sweat. I needed to calm down. I went to the back of Sansone's SUV and found an emergency kit filled with everything from bandages to gauze to tape to peanut butter crackers. I love peanut butter, so I ripped into the crackers. I sat on the side of the highway for a good ten minutes, with the back hatch of the SUV open, while I scarfed down five packages of peanut butter crackers. I couldn't finish them fast enough, my manic urgency controlling every action. I ate them so quickly that I had to root through the car to find a bottle of water so I didn't choke to death.

My heart was beating out of my chest. I was getting dizzy; I needed to lie down. I walked over to the grass to the right of the shoulder, took off all my clothes, lay down, and began making snow angels—or, rather, grass angels—in the freshly cut grass. I flapped my arms and legs for a moment, then stopped to just lie there and look at the moon.

Fuck. It's a full moon tonight.

After a few minutes, I heard a voice.

"Michael . . . Michael . . . Michael?" I stood up and turned around to see JC standing by the car.

"Johnny!"—sometimes I call him that—"Johnny, I am so glad you are okay. You have been passed out for the last couple of hours," I informed him as I stood there in my birthday suit.

"Where the hell are we?" he asked.

"I am not sure," I answered.

"Where are your clothes?" he asked, laughing and smiling.

I guessed. "In the car, I think."

"Where are the keys?" he asked me.

"I don't know."

"Michael! You don't know where the keys are?" I had never heard JC yell at anyone in the ten years I had known him. He is the most laid back person I have ever met. Raising his voice snapped me back into the present and out of the depths of mania.

"Shit, Johnny. I am sorry. They are in my jeans—right behind you, on the seat in the back." I told him.

"Let's get the fuck out of here. Get in!" JC took the keys and drove us thirty minutes south back to Dalhousie.

After fifteen minutes of silence during the drive, I looked down and noticed that I was naked.

"JC, I don't have any clothes on." Mr. Invincible had morphed into Captain Obvious.

"I know, bro. Are you ok?"

"Yeah, hold on and let me put my pants back on." I pulled them on and zipped them up. "Sorry about that, man."

JC knew about my bipolar condition and had other good friends that also battled the disorder, so he knew what was going on, and he reassured me that we were going to be all right.

"Just sit back and relax, Michael. We're going to play Dalhousie tomorrow."

When we finally returned to the campus at Dalhousie, I got out of the car in only my blue jeans. JC went to bed immediately; I tried to, but I tossed and turned in my bed for an hour or so. Restlessness took over my entire body—I couldn't lie there anymore. I twitched, flipped, and fidgeted. I had about two and a half hours to kill before tee time; I needed something to do.

I walked outside and began wandering aimlessly around the Dalhousie property. I took an American flag and switched its position from one cottage to another, then placed a flag of England where the first one had been. Like getting naked on the side if I-55, I have no idea why I needed to switch those flags. They're just bipolar mysteries.

I walked all over the facility for almost two hours. *All of this walking will be good cardio work for Q-School*, I told myself. But then I got my hands on a golf cart and rode down the left side of the driving range, behind the tree line that separated the driving range from the woods. I followed the cart path for about 200 yards, then got out of the cart and threw my brand-new black-and-white Nikes into a pond. Then I hopped back in the golf cart to drive back to the front of the driving range.

I parked the cart near the short-game practice area, grabbed my clubs, and walked directly through three sprinklers to get to the practice putting green. The water slapped my face and drenched my purple Shadow Creek golf shirt.

I hit putts with my sand wedge and chip shots with my putter. All the while, the sprinklers continued to soak me every few minutes. Out of the corner of my eye, I saw people watching me. The golf maintenance staff was already hard at work, and they must have been baffled by my behavior. I didn't see anything wrong with it. After my practice, I needed to change out of the wet clothes.

I returned to the cottage to find all the guys talking about the night before. I retreated to my side of the condo and found a dry outfit. That is when Sansone confronted me.

"Mike, did you take your medicine today?"

"Nick, I actually forgot to bring it with me this weekend." I could never lie to him.

"You're manic, Mike. Do you see that?"

"Nick, do you at least trust me to play this round of golf? I will take my lithium when we get back this afternoon."

"Sure, Mike, but just so you know, you are manic right now." He said in a stern voice.

I will be fine to make it through this round.

* * *

After the word from Nick, I raced to the first tee to join my friends Bill Forrest and Steve Stolze, who were in my threesome. Stolze is a lawyer, a musician, and an entrepreneur. He and I had gone to Cardinal games together but hadn't yet played golf together. What an inaugural round it would be.

Bill Forrest is an entrepreneur in St. Louis, and we share many mutual friends. We had been talking about playing together for years, and we had finally made it happen.

My mind was all over the place during the round. It got to a point where I was just trying to finish, no matter what score I posted. The creeping feeling of being hunted was back.

I kept myself busy in between shots by going over to my playing partners' bags and cleaning their clubs with water and my towel. I was alternating between playing mode and caddie mode. On the thirteenth hole, I sat in my cart and felt the urge to break my cell phone into two pieces so I snapped it in half like a breadstick and threw the pieces into a lake just left of the thirteenth fairway. My playing partners had to have seen me do it. Who knows what they were thinking?

I felt like I was actually playing well, but at the end of the day I had shot a score of 85. It felt like 65. On the last hole of the round, I played my tee shot right of the fairway. It was a wide-open shot of about 235 yards. I took out my nineteen-degree hybrid club and played a shot toward the green. After my ball was well on its way, I turned and softly helicopter-tossed my club into ten-foot tall brush to the right of the final hole. I didn't throw it hard at all, just a gentle toss that landed silently. Then I got in my cart and drove away.

When the round was over, Stolze and Forrest gave me their scorecards; they had to get back to St. Louis. No doubt, they didn't want to hang with me after that manic display. I went out to watch JC, Sansone, Steele, and Gift play their final three holes. After they finished, we all went inside to grab a bite to eat. That is when Sansone told JC he would drive me back to St. Louis. Before we left, I went into the pro shop at Dalhousie and spent a small fortune on shirts, rain pullovers, shoes, and jewelry for my mom. I sent all the charges from my spending spree back to the Missouri Athletic Club, because that was the only way I would be able to cover the $1,100 that I racked up in fifteen minutes.

* * *

Steele, Gift, Sansone, and I hopped into Sansone's silver SUV for the drive. I sat behind the passenger seat, next to Gift, while Steele drove and Sansone rode shotgun. It was ninety-five degrees outside, and I was frantically trying on new long-sleeved rain pullovers one after another.

"Mike, are you okay?" Gift asked me.

"Yeah, Dave. How are you?" I answered with a smile that told Gift that I was not in my right mind.

"I was just checking," he said. My friends had my back as much as they could, but I needed to get control of myself. I was safe in that car with them, but when we got back to St. Louis, I would be on my own, behind the wheel of my Honda.

*   *   *

Sansone dropped me off at JC's house, where I had left my car. I got out of the SUV with my new purchases hanging off my shoulders and grabbed my golf clubs. I looked like a golf octopus moving my clubs from one car to another.

"Mike, go home. I'll call you later, but go home now." Sansone knew I needed to stay in one place.

"Thank you, Nick. Talk to you later," I told him through my driver's side window as he pulled out of the driveway ahead of me. We wound slowly through JC's neighborhood and finally reached a major road. We both turned right on the two-lane street, heading east on Clayton Road, passing Annunziata Church. I moved into the left lane and blew past Nick, doing about sixty miles per hour in a thirty-five-mile-per-hour zone. I was off to the manic races.

Before pulling into my neighborhood, I threw my watch out the driver's side window. I had bought the $110 watch just a few days earlier on another spending spree. A brand new watch, and I just chucked it like my flip phone and my nineteen-degree hybrid club, all for no reason.

When I arrived at my apartment, I went inside and moved pictures to different walls all over the apartment, just as I had done in Pilk's apartment in 2006. I raced to the bathroom and found my pill bottle where I had left it. I took my prescribed four-pill dose. But I was so far gone the lithium would be no help.

I didn't stay at my apartment very long. I noticed that it was five minutes before five, which gave me just enough time to make the five o'clock mass at Mary, Queen of Peace, the church that I grew up in.

I arrived a few minutes after five o'clock. The car ride over was another video game session with my radio buttons. I parked at the east end of Lockwood Boulevard, directly in front of the church, which sits above the road on a big hill. The building was made of light gray stone, with kaleidoscope colored-glass windows and a golden statue of the Virgin Mother Mary on the roof that seemed be ten stories high. It was an impressive building.

I went upstairs to the choir loft. There was no choir for the afternoon service, just a single organist who was laser focused on his playing. I noticed that he looked like Michael J. Fox. I moved to the kneeling bench on the left side of the balcony, knelt down, and took in the service.

Lord, please bless all my family and friends.

I repeated the prayer the entire time I looked out over the people of the parish. The familiarity of the space seemed to slow me down. And, I was running on fumes—I hadn't slept nor eaten anything except peanut butter crackers for a good twenty-four hours.

I crept down the back stairwell of the church and slid out the back door during communion. As I walked down the hill toward my car, a house across the street from the church caught my attention. I could see a trampoline in the backyard. I walked across the street and walked up to the trampoline as if I jumped on it every day. I climbed onto the trampoline and memories of my childhood neighbor's trampoline flooded my mind. My mania had turned me into a ten-year-old kid.

While I was jumping on the trampoline, I noticed that the sky had turned a grayish black, and the wind had picked up so much that the temperature had dropped noticeably. The cool breeze calmed me. After jumping for a few more minutes, I noticed there must have been half a dozen of these cushions scattered all over the brick patio area, all with the letter G stitched in cursive lettering.

What does that G mean on those cushions? Is this God's house? Does that G stand for God?

I was so curious that I got off the trampoline and walked over to the patio. I picked up one of the cushions and studied it. Then I noticed the back door.

God wouldn't mind if I went in his house. Hell, I was just in his house across the street.

I opened the door and walked in to find a living room with couches and a television and a hallway to my left. I followed the hallway to a beautiful kitchen, with black marble countertops and brand-new stainless appliances.

"Can I help you?" A foreign voice rang in my ear.

"Oh, I am just looking for my friend Tony," I said as I walked past a short Italian- looking man and exited the house through the kitchen door onto the driveway. I really wasn't sure why I was there, but I certainly wasn't looking for any Tony.

As I went through the kitchen door, I ran into what must have been his wife and two children. The wife looked frightened. I walked briskly past her and out of the house. As I made my way down the driveway I looked up to see the congregants filing out of church.

The black sky filled with a bright bolt of lightning that lit up the sky as I reached the end of the driveway. It was so bright that it looked like a florescent light. A few seconds later, the most intense crack of thunder cracked, and the skies opened up. I was soaked so quickly that I looked like I had just jumped into a pool.

The thunder and rain scared me; I felt like they were attacking me. I ran to my car, which was only about forty yards away. The raindrops slammed into my body like tiny, powerful explosions. I was drenched and shivering.

When I finally got to the car, I fumbled through both of my pockets; my keys were gone. I stood there for a minute, being pummeled by more rain and the type of thunder that made me flinch with fear.

Fuck the car, I thought. *I will get it later. I have a spare key at home. I can go over to Sweetie's house.*

My grandmother, whom I had called Sweetie since I was a toddler, lived only a few blocks from where I stood in the house my dad grew up in. I could go to her house for shelter from the storm. I jogged through the streets of Webster Groves while lightening lit up the sky. The rain was so heavy that it felt like I was running through a river. Finally, I got to Sweetie's house, across the street from Westborough golf course, where I had learned the game.

I went to the back deck and peered into the square windows that looked into the living room. I didn't see her, and all the doors were locked. Then I noticed her car was gone. I couldn't get into the house, and the rain was still torturing me.

Plan B: Get across the street to the men's locker room at Westborough, I decided. *I have to get out of this hurricane.*

I crossed Berry Road and snuck through the tree line that separated the street from the eleventh hole. I jogged across the fairway and then across the tenth fairway before getting to the back parking lot, where the entrance of the locker room was lit up against the dark storm. I sprinted for the door. I couldn't take the cold rain and the neck-twitching crash of thunder that continued to chase me.

The inside of the locker room was a magnificent sight. Navy blue carpet stretched from wall to wall. The mahogany lockers lined the room. I had been in that locker room hundreds of times. I was at home there.

I went straight for the showers. I turned the hot water on full blast and waited for the shower to warm up. I was freezing, and my teeth were chattering. The hot shower calmed me. I stood in the shower for at least thirty minutes, thinking, praying, worrying, and cleaning myself over and over. Finally, I turned the water off and grabbed two vanilla-colored towels to dry my body.

And then it hit me. *Shit, I don't have any dry clothes! Dad will have something in his locker.*

I made my way to my dad's locker. The only item he had in there was a yellow bathing suit. I put it on; it was too small, but I didn't have another option. I needed a shirt. I strolled through the lockers, looking for a familiar name or an open locker so I could find a shirt. I could bring the shirt back later. I came across Con Lane's locker. He was a close friend of my family. His locker was not locked, and he had left behind a white golf shirt with a blue collar and blazing gold Notre Dame emblem on the chest. I put it on.

I threw my sopping wet clothes and shoes into my dad's locker and left the locker room barefoot. The storm had passed and it had become a beautiful evening. The moon was a perfect crescent shape. I needed to either get to my apartment for the spare car key or figure out how to get inside my car.

The keys could be locked inside the car.

The walk back over the tenth and eleventh fairways to Berry Road was serene. The sky was dark, the moon was bright, and it was around seventy-five degrees. I crossed Berry Road and made my way to the back entrance to Mary, Queen of Peace's grade school. As I walked through the parking lot toward the church, memories of wonderful days playing soccer on the blacktop of that parking lot during recess flashed through my memory.

I walked through the opening that separated the school and the church. When I turned the corner, I saw my dad sitting on the steps of the church with a cell phone in his hand. My phone was at the bottom of a lake in Cape Girardeau, and Dad hadn't been able to reach me. He had seen my car in front of the church and had stopped to look for me. I felt a weight lifted from my back when I saw him on the church steps.

"Michael! Where have you been?" He greeted me with a smile and a handshake.

"I was over at Westborough," I said. I tried to play it off like I was fine, but being barefoot didn't help me convince him.

"Your mom is down by your car," he informed me. "Let's go."

We walked down the hill to my Honda.

"Michael, what happened to your mirror?" my mom asked, as she greeted me with a warm hug.

"I don't know, Mom. I really don't know." I was delirious.

"Where are your keys?"

"I don't know, Mom. I really don't know." Still delirious.

We all got in my dad's blue Jeep and drove off in silence. When we got to my apartment, the power was out from the earlier storm, so we lit candles to see. My mom found the shattered car mirror on the kitchen counter where I had left it.

"Let's go home," my dad instructed. He had found my lithium on the bathroom counter and put it in his pocket.

* * *

We had a bite to eat in the kitchen, and eventually, I retreated to the basement, where I had spent many nights watching old videotapes of college basketball games and old Masters tournaments. The basement was my safe place.

I parked myself on the couch and turned on ESPN. I fidgeted and squirmed on the couch for a good hour and a half until the fidgeting turned into paranoia. I found an old baseball under the couch and walked into the furnace room, which had two small windows.

I started getting that feeling of being hunted. *You'll never catch me.*

I threw the baseball as hard as I could at the window on the right. The glass shattered everywhere. As I sprinted from the room, I stepped on a piece of glass, which lodged in my right foot.

I ran as fast as I could up the basement stairs. As I reached the top, I had a sudden sensation of terror, like a young kid alone in the dark. Chills ran down my back. I was on a mad dash to get out of the house before anyone or anything could get me. I dashed out the side door of the house slamming it behind me. I ran full steam down my parents' street to Berry Road. I took a right turn onto Berry and headed south in a full sprint. I made another right at the first street, Berrywood Drive. Something was chasing me.

I ducked behind the third house on the right and climbed under a car in the driveway.

If I stay still and quiet, they won't find me.

I stayed there for a good ten minutes before realizing that my foot was bleeding from stepping on the shattered glass. I climbed out from under the car and briefly thought I was safe. But that feeling of safety quickly vanished. I once again needed to take off all my clothes, so I shed the yellow bathing suit and the Notre Dame shirt and headed back to Berry Road with no clothes on.

I only made it about five hundred yards before the Glendale Police Department found me. The lights of the police SUV were a welcome sight, a beacon of safety.

"Son, are you okay?" The policeman asked me.

"I don't think so," I admitted as I leaned on the hood of the SUV.

"Why don't you hop in the backseat, and I can get you home."

"Sounds good to me." I wasted no time in getting into the back.

I sat in the car for a good twenty minutes before the cop got back in and drove me back to my parents' house. My mom and dad were waiting in the driveway when we pulled up. As I got out of the SUV with no clothes on I saw the fear on my parents' faces. I was embarrassed and raced inside to find some clothes.

When I came back outside, the police SUV was pulling away. My dad told me to get in the backseat of his car.

"Michael, get in here," he instructed, as if I were three years old.

I didn't argue. My dad drove, my mom next to him in the front seat. The uncomfortable silence filled every inch of the car. I didn't know where we were going. I sat in the back and looked out the window at the crescent moon. Eventually, we pulled up to the emergency room at Barnes–Jewish Hospital.

* * *

When they brought me in, the nurses took my vitals and realized that they needed to slow down my heart rate. My ticker was pounding like a rabbit's. They took me into a small room—I trailed blood across the floor from the open cut on my foot—and hooked me up to some sort of machine. I had no clue what it was doing to me.

After about twenty minutes, the nurses returned me to the small holding cell in the bowels of the hospital. I had been in the same room one year earlier, almost to the day. This time, my mom came with me into the tiny white room. It was her first look at the cell, where I would be imprisoned until being taken to the psychiatric floor. The skinny white mattress was still on the floor; I climbed onto it while my mom sat quietly in the corner. I was exhausted and lost. After lying there for a few minutes, everything hit me at once.

I'm back in the hospital again? How can I be here again?

I began to cry. It was the type of deep cry where you feel like you're choking. I couldn't control the tears. I couldn't catch my breath. My mom held me in her arms like she did when I was a toddler and comforted me.

"Shhh, shhh, Michael. You are going to be fine. I am right here."

The emotion was so intense that I wept until I passed out.

* * *

When I awoke, I found myself in a room on the fifteenth floor again. The familiar sour bleach smell stung my nostrils.

I had been pumped full of drugs to even me out and had been asleep for more than forty-eight hours. It was September 6.

Fifteen days to Q-School. I need to get the fuck out of here. Am I really here . . . again?

Dr. Cloninger was the first person I saw when I walked out of my room. I was relieved to see him; it was rare for him to be on this floor. In all my days and nights on the fifteenth floor, I had only seen Cloninger three times before this visit.

"Michael, let's sit down in here." He brought me into a tiny room with a chair and a loveseat and closed the door behind us.

"Doc, what am I doing in here again?" I pleaded. "I haven't been drinking at all."

"Were you off your medicine?"

"I was off of it for about two days," I admitted. "But I was off of it for around forty days back in February and March."

"Well, that is a perfect example of just how powerful bipolar disorder can be. One forty-eight-hour lapse in your routine can wind you up in here," he told me.

I thought I had been doing everything right. But without the medication in my system, the disorder had spun me around in just a matter of hours.

"Remember: The last time we talked, you were thinking about switching medications from the lithium to lamotrigine. Would you still be interested in trying that?"

"Yes! Yes! I need a fresh start. What are the side effects?"

"Nothing you can't handle. Headaches may be a factor for the first two weeks, but those should go away after your body metabolizes the lamotrigine. The only other side effect is that you will feel some itching, similar to having a rash on your skin, for the first two weeks, but that will go away eventually, too," he advised.

"Alright, Doc. I am in for the new medicine. Now—how long before I get out of here?"

"I want to keep you for seven days and make sure you are stable, and then you can go. So I want you here for another week."

I did the math in my head.

Seven days would get me out of here on September 13. That means I would be out in time to play in the money game at Boone Valley on the seventeenth, and I can get to Dallas by the nineteenth, which would give me time to prepare for Q-School on the twenty-first.

"Okay, Doc. I can handle seven days." I was back in my right mind: The sedatives and two days of sleep had buried my mania.

* * *

Those seven days on the fifteenth floor were the easiest I have ever done in Barnes. I even called Sansone to tell him where I was.

"Nick, I am at the hospital getting my oil changed, but I will be out in time for your golf event at your club," I said to his voice mail.

I spent the next week listening to different types of music during my music-therapy hours, and I made bracelets for my mom and sister during arts and crafts sessions. I played pool and Ping-Pong. I checked my email and sent out messages to a few people, letting them know where I was and that I was focusing on getting better. It was basically like indoor camp.

The new medication was working: I felt the headaches and the itchiness on my skin, but my mind was moving slower. I was more thoughtful. I could handle headaches and itching if my mind stayed at an even keel. Physical pain could mostly be ignored while I created a new awareness between my ears.

Eight days to Q-School.

* * *

I locked myself into three days of practice before the Boone Valley event, but I was focused on Q-School.

The Golf Club of Dallas sits in the heart of the city. All the greats from the state of Texas have played there: Nelson, Hogan, Trevino, Wadkins. It is a Perry Maxwell design—a collaboration with his son, and his final work before he died in 1952. There is history at this golf course, and I was excited to play it.

It was Q-School. The pressure of tournament golf was pumping adrenaline through my body for the next few days. I had been taking the lamotrigine every morning now as part of my routine, and my equilibrium and balance were knocked loose from all the medications that were pumped into me back in the hospital. When I stood over the golf ball, it felt like I was trying to stand on an inner tube that was floating in a pool. But after a few days of practice I felt more like myself, and my balance returned.

The first competitive round of the event was on Wednesday, the twenty-first. On the twentieth, I went to the parking lot for a practice round and to find a caddie.

"Say, man. You need a loop?" asked a man in a University of Texas baseball cap. He had to be close to my age. Blonde hair leaked from the ball cap and covered his ears.

"Yes! I need a loop badly. You open this week?"

"Yes, sir," he said in that Texas drawl.

I introduced myself. "First of all, don't call me sir. My name is Mike."

"I have been caddying for a long time," he told me.

"You loop for anyone I may know?" I asked.

He answered. "David Gossett."

My golf history mind went to work and remembered that David Gossett had shot 59 at the Q-School in the past and had also won the US Amateur. I was sold right there.

"What's your name?" I asked.

"Lanny Brown." He said.

One day until Q-School.

* * *

Lanny met me on the range around 7:15 a.m. I was fired up.

The opening tee shot at any Q-School is always a mental challenge. I visualized my customary high cut shot and played my ball to the center of the fairway. I had 138 yards left to the hole in the middle of the green. I felt the Q-School juice running through my entire body. It was marvelous. I chose a wedge for my second shot. I made a solid swing and had fifteen feet left for an opening birdie. I two-putted to get my sea legs underneath me. We were off and running.

I played solidly through my first round and posted a 70 in twenty to twenty-five mile per hour Texas winds. It was a solid round, and it gave me a positive charge.

When I woke up on the morning of the second round, I felt sluggish. I felt down. I began feeling the effects of a depressive cycle that always follows a manic episode. When I got to the course, I wasn't nervous. The depression had silenced my nerves again.

If you aren't nervous on the first tee of a tournament . . . something is wrong.

I posted a sloppy 74, but it could easily have been much higher. I was at 144 after two rounds and inside the cut by one stroke heading to the final day. The new Q-School criteria made this stage only a three-round event.

As soon as the second round was over, I went to a health club that I frequented whenever I was in Dallas, The Verandah Club. When I arrived in the parking lot, my sluggishness had progressed so far that I was almost physically unable to get out of my car. I made it into the health club and threw myself on a treadmill. I needed to get my endorphins working to counteract my depressive feelings. It was difficult to keep going, but I forced myself to run on the treadmill for thirty-five minutes and then do push-ups and core exercises. By the end of the workout, I felt in a much better place mentally. It was clear proof of how exercise, one of the Fourteen Clubs can help you beat depression.

The morning of the final round started off badly when I broke my cell phone by knocking it off my nightstand. Not having a cell phone wouldn't hinder my play directly (I always leave my phone in my car when I am at the golf course), but it was another thing to occupy my mind and worry about taking care of later. I woke up with enough time to return to The Verandah Club before the final round; I wanted to loosen up my body and get my blood pumping. I wasn't going to make the same mistake that I made the day before by not warming up properly.

By the time I finished my morning workout, my body was flowing with positive endorphins. My muscles were warm and ready to go. I was nervous on the way to the golf course, my heart rate was up, and I loved it. I listened to Pearl Jam in the car to get my mind where it needed to be.

Lanny met me in the parking lot, and we walked to the range together.

I felt so lucky to be playing this round of golf; ten days earlier, I'd had needles in my arms.

My warm up on the course was marvelous. I found my rhythm and tempo after only five swings, and I was ready to go. We stopped by the putting green to hit practice putts, and I was struck with an idea. I had putted so poorly the day before that I decided I would putt this round with my eyes closed. I had used the technique a year before with great success, but in the twelve months since, I had changed my putting routine. I had missed so many putts the day before because I was tentatively guiding putts toward the hole instead of freely hunting the hole. I needed to free myself up; I decided there was nothing more freeing than closing your eyes and letting go. The first few putts on the practice green with my eyes closed found the bottom of the hole. I hit a few long putts, and my speed was spot on. I committed to it right there: eyes closed all day today.

Those nerves—they can be both good and bad—jumped up and bit me on my opening tee shot of the day. I sliced it to the far right side of the hole, and it looked as though my ball was going to go out of bounds. It landed only a few yards in bounds, but I had a shot. I channeled my best Seve Ballesteros and played a low hooking four-iron shot under some trees and bounced my ball up near the green from 189 yards. The shot landed in a green-side bunker, from where I made a lucky bogey to start the round; my tee shot should have gone out of bounds. I made par on numbers eleven, twelve, and thirteen. At number fourteen, I made a six-footer for my first birdie of the day after playing a marvelous bump-and-run shot between two green-side bunkers on the par five. Now I had momentum.

"Atta boy, Pro. Do you think the Cowboys can cover this weekend?" Lanny knew the momentum had just swung in our favor, so he kept my mind off the pressure by asking a gambling question—great caddying.

The fifteenth hole at the Golf Club of Dallas is a medium-length dog-leg-left par four; I selected a one iron and tried to shape it from right to left in order to find the fairway, but the wind was behind us, and I misjudged my club selection. I pulled the shot to the left and wound up in the rough with 134 yards to the hole, cut at the bottom of a steep slope. The distance between my ball and the hole stretched downhill and away from me, and there was water only five yards from the hole. My first instinct was, of course, awful. Bipolar disorder was rearing its head.

I got nothing with this shot . . . Damn it, don't let the bipolar disorder let you think that way—I GOT this shot.

I had so many options. The ball was sitting on a mixture of hardpan and mulch. There were pinecones everywhere around my ball, so I moved them out of the way. I could play an eight or a six iron for this shot; I could putt it; I could use a hybrid club . . . The shot was so difficult that I had literally seven different club options. I finally chose my fifty-two-degree wedge.

I channeled Seve again and played a short chip shot that landed only a few feet in front of me, took a few soft bounces over the sandy hardpan and mulch, landed in the rough, and then crept onto the fringe of the green and almost stopped dead . . . then started speeding up again as it reached the surface of the green. It trundled down the slope toward the hole, took a peek in the left side of the cup, and just hung there, only inches away.

It was far and away the greatest short-game shot that I have ever played in my life. The golf gods had touched me before I hit the ball. I'm sure I will never play a better short-game shot as long as I live.

I tapped in for par while still holding my fifty-two-degree wedge. That shot was more momentum on top of the mojo from the birdie on the previous hole. I made par on the next two holes and scrambled for another good bogey on number eighteen—my ninth hole of the day.

Nine strong holes and I'll make the cut.

I made three pars in a row to begin my final nine of the tournament. I finally made another birdie on the thirteenth hole of the day. I knew I was going to be right around the cut number. I made two clutch, eyes-closed, eight-foot putts for par on the next two holes, and I was ready to go down the stretch. My fifteenth hole of the round would be the toughest hole on the entire course. It was a 470-yard par four into the wind. Lanny knew the hole well.

"Pro, if you take a driver over those trees on the right side, you will have a perfect angle to the green." He was pointing me fifty yards right of the fairway.

"Over there?" I said in disbelief.

"Yeah, Pro. That's the spot."

"All right, partner. You got it," I confirmed.

I hit my biggest drive of the day exactly where he told me. Sure enough, there was a big opening on that side that looked right at the green. We had

185 yards to the hole and 184 to the front edge of the green. I was jacked up on adrenaline and chose my eight iron. It was the right club, and my approach landed pin high about twenty-five feet left of the hole. I two-putted for a par that felt like a birdie.

One shot at a time.

My sixteenth hole was an uphill par three that played 191 yards to a multiterraced green. The hole was cut on the middle tier, precariously close to the slope that would bring any errant shot back to the front of the green, more than thirty feet from the hole.

I caught my tee shot a bit heavy and the ball came up on the front of the green, with forty feet left for birdie. I managed a solid putt under the circumstances and left myself six feet to save par. I pulled the par putt badly and missed for a bogey.

One shot at a time.

I worked out some of my angst with my driver on the next tee shot by hitting a long, arcing bomb. I was left with eighty-nine yards into the par four. I hit my approach over the green to the back fringe and had another forty-foot-birdie chance. The putt was diabolical. It would be coming out of the fringe and needed to cover the first thirty feet before it went uphill to a hole cut on the top of a shelf. I read the putt from every angle. I went through my routine, closed my eyes, and let the putt go. I never looked up and didn't open my eyes until I heard Lanny.

"Amazing putt, Pro! Great birdie!" His voice muffled the clapping of a few spectators.

We went into the final hole with a head of steam. My adrenaline was spiking at this point. I decided that I would play a three wood on my final tee shot, because a driver with this type of adrenaline would be too much power. My shot found the fairway, and I was left with 148 yards to the hole. It was a perfect knock-down nine-iron shot with the adrenaline factor. I executed well and played to the fat side of the green, and my ball finished fifteen feet left of the hole. It would be a very good look at birdie. I went through my routine, closed my eyes, and let the putt go. It missed to the left. I tapped in for a final round of 70 and would have to wait about three hours to find out my fate. I had a three-day total of 214.

* * *

"You sure are fun to work for," Lanny said as we walked to the parking lot after signing the scorecard.

"Thanks, man. You were a great loop," I said. "Can you be available for the next stage of qualifying?"

"I think you are gonna make it through today, so give me a call and let me know where you play next," he said.

As I put my clubs and shoes in my trunk, I remembered that I didn't have a cell phone. I would have to stop on my way back to St. Louis. There was no reason to stay in Dallas, no playoffs at Q-School. I would either be in for the next qualifying round or I wouldn't.

So I hopped in my Honda and headed north on I-75. In Plano, just north of Dallas, I saw a sign for my cell phone provider, so I pulled off the freeway. The customer service rep listened to my quandary and tried to help, but he was out of the phone model that fit my plan. I told him that I was heading north to St. Louis, and he gave me an address in Tulsa for a sister store. The store in Tulsa was the only one between Dallas and St. Louis that had my phone in stock. The drive from Dallas to Tulsa would be four long hours.

So many thoughts ran through my head during that four-hour drive.

I am going to qualify. When I get to Tulsa, I am going to get my phone and call Dad, and he is going to tell me that I qualified.

The ride was up and down, like a bipolar rollercoaster ride.

If I don't make it through qualifying . . . what am I going to do?

I made it through. The birdie on the second-to-last hole got me in.

Every minute seemed like an hour. Normally, a four-hour car ride was a walk in the park for me, but this one was an eternity. My entire year was at stake. I looked at the odometer; I had put 38,761 miles on my car in only eleven months.

When I finally got to Tulsa, my cell phone provider had the phone waiting for me; the sales rep in Dallas had called ahead and reserved it. They activated my new phone. As soon as the phone was up and running, I saw an incoming call from the 312 area code—a Chicago number. It was my friend Dan Jermak, a big supporter of my career.

"Danny, I haven't had a phone for the last four hours. Do you know if I made it through the Dallas qualifier?" I crossed my fingers.

He broke the news. "Missed by one."

"Wow." My heart sunk into the pit of my stomach.

I remembered all the putts that I had missed the entire week that could have saved that one shot. I recalled being lazy and not getting my endorphins up at the gym before the second round. I thought about my parents, who always rooted for me. I had planned on calling Mr. Anonymous to tell him that I made it through, but now I couldn't do that. It wasn't the first time that year that one shot cost me, but it was still demoralizing. I turned the phone off for the rest of the ride back to St. Louis.

* * *

When I finally got back into St. Louis, I was sitting at a red light on Big Bend Road where it meets Highway 44 when my mind began bouncing around.

One shot—unbelievable. I didn't play badly. I was right there until the very end.

I was trying to squeeze something positive out of the situation, as Brian Cain might have. And then a thought jumped into my head that had never ever been there before.

You should just kill yourself. You can just drive the car off the road into a cement wall. That would solve all of this.

I let the thought process.

Then I broke into hysterical laughter. It was a cackle of disbelief that this thought would go through my brain. That's not who I am, not how I have been taught to live my life. Killing myself would mean that I was a quitter. I don't quit—ever. Where did that thought come from if not from me?

"You have got to be kidding me!" I screamed in my car.

I had a revelation: The bipolar disorder was trying to kill me.

Now I was pissed off. I was healthy—disappointed about the golf tournament, sure—but I was physically fit, on my meds, and playing damn well. All the one-stroke misses during the course of the year had taught me not to allow my golf results to bother me. At thirty-three years old, I had finally learned that my golf was only a game and that my health was much more important. As I drove down Big Bend, I had my first and last conversation with bipolar disorder. I was healthy, so I was able to realize that the disorder was producing those suicidal thoughts.

You think you can kill me? Rage filled my body. *Not if I kill you first.*

At that moment, I tried to find the equivalent of suicide in tournament golf. It would be like walking off the golf course if your round wasn't going well and not turning in a scorecard. Suicide would be like walking off the golf course of life. I would never walk off the golf course before completing a tournament round. I was always taught that you turn in your scorecard no matter what your score. It's a privilege to play a tournament round of golf; some may even call it a gift. To walk off the golf course is unacceptable, against everything that I have ever been taught about life and golf. Thank goodness for golf, or I may have walked off the golf course of life right then and there. I was always taught to respect the game of golf. It took bipolar disorder to help me truly respect the game of life.

THE FOURTEEN CLUBS

After my brush with suicidal thoughts, I vowed to continue my medication, with no more lapses—ever. I worked out what it would take for me to permanently keep bipolar disorder at bay, to avoid mania, and conquer depression. I used my experience and what I'd learned from teachers like Brian Cain and Dr. Cloninger, from group and music therapy, and created the Fourteen Clubs. I hope my story will lead others with bipolar disorder to use the Fourteen Clubs to find a healthy balance in their own lives.

THE FOURTEEN CLUBS

THE BIPOLAR MIND has an extra gear: It works faster and is capable of more than the average mind. When it is fed properly, it can do great things. I try to incorporate these tools, which I call the *Fourteen Clubs*, to support my bipolar mind. A tournament golfer is allowed fourteen clubs to compete against the golf course, and these Fourteen Clubs can be used to compete against bipolar disorder every day.

My respect for and integrity with the rules of golf helped me to understand that I needed to follow certain rules in order to remain healthy off the golf course. Golf and bipolar disorder are similar in that neither can ever be completely mastered. They are both a daily challenge. The lessons that I have learned from the game have aided me in keeping the disorder at arm's length, but bipolar disorder is a daily battle very similar to teeing off in a brand-new round of golf. There are birdies to be made every day. The bogeys will always lurk, but the Fourteen Clubs can help the bipolar mind make more birdies than bogeys each day.

MEDICATION

First, and foremost, a person with bipolar disorder must commit to taking his or her medicine. The bipolar mind must be dedicated, willing to compete every day against the disorder. Otherwise, it will win, which could cost you your life. Taking meds daily is the first step toward a victory against the disorder. I definitely experimented with not using medication enough times to realize that life on medication is a much more stable existence.

The one common denominator in the lead-up to all my hospital stays was not having enough medication in my system. Medication works. Choosing to not take medicine is a serious gamble. I gambled many times and always lost. If it is possible to take your meds at the same time every day, that would aid the bipolar mind in feeling a sense of routine (see "Routine and Gratitude").

I find that many people are afraid to take or try meds. The thought process is always the same with these people: They come up with negative reasons to avoid taking medicine; my recommendation is to consider the positives. Medications are designed to improve quality of life and have been proven to do so. If you come across a medication that doesn't agree with you, don't be afraid to try another. Work on a treatment plan with your doctor, and use medication to your advantage. The correct medication slows down the bipolar mind. When the bipolar mind can remain slow and methodical, it will be healthy and can achieve amazing things. The bipolar mind is a tremendous engine. I consider the correct medication to be the oil in that engine.

EXERCISE

Exercise is imperative and the most lethal tool for staving off depressed feelings. Exercise is real-life magic for the bipolar brain. Obviously, long and elaborate workouts are great, but even small, fifteen- to thirty-minute workouts can change the direction of the bipolar mind. It doesn't matter whether you run, swim, bike, dance, lift weights, or walk.

You may need to push yourself to get an exercise routine started. Instead of doing a big workout once a week, try smaller workouts three to five times a week. Three twenty-minute workouts in a week will be more effective against bipolar disorder than a single two-hour workout per week. Those small workouts bring about positive endorphins, which keep the mood level or even lift it.

However, of course, too much of anything is never good. A day of rest in between workouts can be just as important as the workouts themselves. The bipolar mind is famous for trying to do everything at once. When you learn to space things out, mood consistency is more attainable. There are three certainties in life: death, taxes, and that you will always feel better after a workout than you did before the workout. If you can afford to invest in a personal trainer or specific fitness classes, that is money well spent!

ADEQUATE SLEEP AND REST

Bipolar disorder has cost me a lot of sleep. At certain points in my life, not sleeping for two weeks at a time was not uncommon. It took me years to realize that it was the illness that kept me awake all of those nights in my teenage years.

Sleep and rest are essential in the battle with bipolar disorder. You must rest the brain. Naps are a great tool to help ease the body and mind.

During the production of this book, for the first time in my life, I felt mania coming on before it took over. In the past, I was unaware until I was deep within it, but I had created a new awareness about my own mania through maintaining consistent sleep patterns. When I felt the mania surge, I took naps for two days in a row—just short, forty-five-minute naps. They worked, and it only took two days to rebalance and keep the mania away.

The healthiest place for someone with bipolar to sleep is a room where natural light comes in at daybreak. Try your best not to sleep with the television on; that is not quality sleep.

My mood fluctuates more if I get less than six hours of sleep per night. I would love it if life allowed me to get seven or eight hours of quality sleep every night, but that's just not always possible. A nap can help make up the difference. Proper rest creates important balance for the bipolar mind and body. The bipolar mind can move at such a breakneck pace that it sometimes literally forgets about rest. Don't underestimate the importance of resting on your couch while watching TV or a good movie. Realize that there are specific ways to relax in order to recharge your mind's batteries: massage, manicures and pedicures, yoga, meditation, quiet reading, going to see a new film at the theatre. Rest is needed just as much as medication in the battle against bipolar disorder.

HEALTHY DIET

Food goes a long way in the battle against bipolar disorder. Mentally, it is good for the mind to know that the body has been fed with foods that are healthy and beneficial. Lean protein, vegetables, fish, and fruit are excellent food choices, and water and orange juice will keep you hydrated. I have learned that brown rice is a healthy energy source when I'm running low.

When the bipolar mind knows and feels that the proper food has been put into the body, it aids the mind in feeling healthy on a psychological level as well. When the bipolar mind moves too fast, it causes the mind to literally forget to eat. Make mealtime a staple in your routine to nourish both body and mind.

It takes serious discipline to make the correct food choices. On the flip side, if the bipolar mind knows that the body has been fed poorly, it can lead to depression. And bipolar depression is to be avoided at all costs.

However, a cheat day here and there is also good for the soul!

THERAPY

There are many people out there who act tough and say they don't need therapy. Others will tell me they can't afford therapy. I will tell them that therapy doesn't have to be with a mental health professional. You can have a therapy session with anyone that you trust.

If you trust someone, you can talk about your mood with them, and they can offer suggestions and ideas for you to consider. Talking through what you are feeling with a friend can be as beneficial as seeing a professional therapist.

When I first began therapy, I didn't learn anything. I would go in and sit down, face to face with my doctors, and I would talk, but I didn't listen. Finally, I began to approach therapy sessions as a time to grow and learn, to improve myself. The bipolar mind can slip into the *I know everything* mode, and that mind-set is detrimental to learning anything.

Therapy with a mental health professional is certainly encouraged and can open doors that you never knew existed. I view the mind as another muscle. You must help that muscle to grow and become stronger by nourishing it properly. Therapy nourishes the bipolar mind. I find that exchanging phone calls, emails, and text messages with trusted friends and family can serve as effective therapy as well.

MUSIC THERAPY

Music therapy is absolutely essential in combatting bipolar disorder every day. I am not musically inclined. I can't read music, and I don't play a musical instrument—not one. But as a person who has learned to be more self-aware, I must credit music therapy as a powerful partner in my own fight against bipolar disorder.

I would advise incorporating music into your life as much as possible: when you are in your car, when you are getting ready for work, when you are working out, when you are preparing dinner, when you are doing yard work. Music has the ability to make the hair on the back of your neck stand up. That kind of power can be used to fight bipolar depression.

Going to watch live music is a therapy session in itself. New music can really bolster energy. Whether it's brand new music on the radio or older music that you hear for the first time, music is a perfect tool to battle any type of depression. Music can change your mood instantaneously, and when combatting a mood disorder, music is a tremendous weapon.

ROUTINE AND GRATITUDE

It has taken me years to understand the importance of routine and gratitude. Life has a way of knocking you out of your routine unless you are committed to it. Once I learned the power of gratitude, I made it part of my everyday routine.

As a tournament golfer, I rely on my preshot routine. In my life off the golf course, the equivalent to my preshot routine would be taking my meds every morning when I wake up. That's what works best for me. After I take my meds, I try to incorporate all the Fourteen Clubs the best I can into every single day.

Routine can include things like waking up at the same time every day, going to the gym at the same time, eating a similar lunch each day, showering at the same time every day, and taking medication at the same time every day. It's not essential to do things at the same time each day but it can help. Routine aids in getting things organized. The bipolar mind needs all the help it can get when organizing, and routine is another secret weapon.

Once I incorporated taking notice of gratitude into my routine, it opened up a new dimension in my own bipolar mind. I began to feel gratitude for many small things: food to eat, a car to drive, a roof over my head, family and friends that care for me. You must be willing to ask yourself, *What am I truly grateful for today?* Feeling grateful for everything you have helps the bipolar mind because without gratitude, the bipolar brain will find a way to focus on things that are missing. Gratitude is a lifestyle, not just a once-in-a-while thing. I try to feel gratitude at least once a day as part of my routine. I may write down what I am grateful for or I may offer up a quiet thank you in my own mind for all the things that I am grateful to enjoy, big or small. I can promise one thing: The bipolar mind works much better when it feels gratitude every day. It can replace the selfishness that bipolar disorder creates. Gratitude is magic.

WATER

One of the worst feelings brought on by bipolar disorder is the dreaded bipolar depression. Dehydration leads to fatigue, which can trigger this depression. Making a conscious effort to drink more water can help fend off depression's lurking spell. You simply can't drink enough water. It's also a mental pat on the back every time you drink water instead of having that extra beer or soft drink.

SOCIAL INTERACTION

Bipolar disorder is the most selfish of diseases. The disorder has the ability to make a person who lives with it feel like they are on an island. Being around people in public can remove that feeling of seclusion. Taking in live sporting events, going to the movies, going out to dinner, shopping and visiting with friends can aid this "stranded on an island" feeling.

THE FIVE SENSES

Getting in touch with all five senses can help the bipolar mind create new awareness, which bipolar disorder can rob you of. Stimulating all five senses heightens your awareness. Pay attention to the fives senses more often, and the bipolar mind can be more free. The bipolar mind works best when it is free, but without awareness, that mind can get tangled. Heightening the five senses every day can create the freedom for a stable bipolar mind.

CLEAN ORGANIZATION

The bipolar mind functions best when it is organized. Cleaning and organizing different things can set the bipolar mind at ease. Cleaning a bedroom, a bathroom, an office, a desk, or any living quarters gives the bipolar mind a sense of organization and cleanliness. A simple act like going to the car wash aids the bipolar mind in feeling a fresh start. The bipolar mind can get cluttered and messy, but cleaning and organizing things at home or at work can give you a sense of accomplishment that can be part of a weekly or monthly routine.

SENSE OF HUMOR

The bipolar mind has a unique ability to make someone take themselves too seriously. Having a sense of humor about the disease can help anyone who lives with it. The ability to recognize that bipolar disorder can and will make you do some strange things will help anyone deal with the condition. When a bipolar sufferer learns to make fun of themselves about some of the quirky behavior that bipolar disorder produces, life can be a lot easier. But sometimes it's difficult for the bipolar mind to have that sense of humor, because the intensity of the disease makes the mind so serious. Learn to make fun of yourself a little more, and you can beat the disorder more easily.

READING

The bipolar mind gets in trouble when it is stagnant and lazy. Reading exercises the mind and keeps the bipolar brain moving. Just as people need to exercise their bodies to beat bipolar disorder, the mind must be exercised as well. Becoming a voracious reader gives the bipolar mind an edge against the disorder. Quiet time for reading can also provide another avenue to relax the mind and quiet the bipolar fire.

FAITH MEDITATION

I don't care if you go to a Jewish Synagogue, a Buddhist Temple, a Catholic Church or a park bench near a nice body of water, but finding a quiet place to meditate or pray will assuredly aid the bipolar mind in finding balance. Get in touch with whatever higher power you believe in and make these meditation sessions a part of your routine. It doesn't have to be for hours on end; even just ten or fifteen minutes per day can provide more balance. Relaxing the bipolar mind with quiet prayer or meditation is a most useful tool in defeating the disorder. Use them to your advantage.

ABOUT THE AUTHOR

MICHAEL WELLINGTON IS a native of St. Louis, Missouri. He is a mental health activist, public speaker, broadcaster, consultant, and professional golfer. He is the founder and chairman of birdies4bipolar.org, an organization that helps raise awareness and funding for mental health. He lives in Palm Beach Gardens, Florida.